The
Iowa
Writers'
Workshop

Stephen Wilbers

The IOWA WRITERS' WORKSHOP

Origins, Emergence, & Growth

Iowa City University of Iowa Press

University of Iowa Press, Iowa City 52242
© 1980 by The University of Iowa
Printed in the United States of America

Library of Congress Cataloging in Publication Data
Wilbers, Stephen, 1949–
    The Iowa Writers' Workshop.

    Bibliography: p.
    Includes index.
    1. Iowa Writers' Workshop.   I.   Title.
PN181.W5   810'.6'0777   80–20190
ISBN 0–87745–098–6
ISBN 0–87745–105–2 (pbk.)

Contents

To Deb

I

ORIGINS

Regionalism

REGIONALISM was the significant literary influence during the Workshop's emergence at the University of Iowa. Simply defined, it was an early twentieth-century literary movement that advocated pride in locale. Particularly evident in the South and the Midwest, regionalism encouraged writers to turn to their own environments for material and to rebel against the predominating cultural influence of the East.

The midwestern regionalist movement, for which Iowa City became a center, began to take shape just before the turn of the century. Before then, Iowa's artists and writers seemed eager to escape the confines of their homeland in search of "worthy" material. Convinced of the inadequacy or even non-existence of their regional culture, they failed to recognize the value and uniqueness of the life around them.[1] The result, according to later Iowa authors like Ruth Suckow and Wallace Stegner, was that the indigenous culture of the pioneer state was generally disregarded. It was this attitude, they felt, combined with a Puritanic distrust of art when art is produced and enjoyed for its own sake, that was responsible for the dearth of literary activity in early Iowa.

But in the 1890s a new interest in writing began to manifest itself and clusters of writers could be found in various areas across the state. Gathered in the Mississippi River town of Davenport, where literary discussion societies like the Contemporary Club were thriving, were Alice French (Octave Thanet), Susan Glaspell, George Cram Cook, Harry Hansen, Arthur Davison Ficke, Cornelia Lynde Meigs, and Floyd Dell. Some fifty miles to the west of Davenport in the small university town of Iowa City, the first of a long succession of writers' clubs was founded. Still farther west in the city of Des Moines, the *Midland Monthly*, which was to be "distinctively a magazine of the Middle-West and the North-West,"[2] had been established by Johnson Brigham.

By the turn of the century, Iowa authors were writing about Iowa. This shift was an extension of the local color movement, a national trend toward preoccupation with locality. Like Bret Harte in the West, Sarah Orne Jewett in New England, Kate Chopin in Louisiana, and Samuel Clemens in

California and on the Mississippi, midwestern authors like Hamlin Garland, Zona Gale, Emerson Hough, and Herbert Quick began writing about their region and attending to the material at hand. No longer were Iowa authors so sensitive to eastern concerns and opinion and no longer were they blind to the worth of their unique environment. Iowa culture, which hitherto had been dressed in the "third hand garments" of the East, was now—in the words of Ruth Suckow—an "awkward, growing young creature" that "could no longer attempt to hide his big hands and feet" and "either had to shut itself up or appear in homemade clothes."[3]

Paradoxically, the regionalist movement in Iowa City was given impetus by a Harvard philosopher who was visiting the University as a guest speaker. On June 10, 1902, Josiah Royce delivered an address entitled "Provincialism" to the Phi Beta Kappa Society of the University of Iowa. By providing a cogent argument for pride in locale, the speech reinforced and perhaps crystalized an attitude that shaped literary developments in Iowa City for the next three decades.

Josiah Royce defined "province" not as a milieu with qualities opposite those of the city, but as "any one part of a national domain, which is, geographically and socially, sufficiently unified to have a true consciousness of its own unity, to feel a pride in its own ideals and customs, and to possess a sense of its distinction from other parts of the country."[4] He argued that "provincialism," or "the love and pride which leads the inhabitants of a province" to cherish their own "customs and ideals," offered a "saving power" both to the modern individual who was threatened by the loss of his self-consciousness and dignity, and to the nation, which was in danger of losing its humanity and so becoming an "incomprehensible monster."[5]

In the State of Iowa, as in Iowa City, there were indications of a new commitment to native culture. On October 5, 6, and 7, 1914, the "Iowa Authors' Homecoming" was held in Des Moines in an "effort to restore the balance of emphasis in the life of the state" and to show other states that Iowa had books other than "a bulging pocket book and an agricultural report."[6] Among the authors participating were Harvey Ingham, Hamlin Garland, Arthur Davison Ficke, Major S. H. M. Byers, Lewis Worthington Smith, Alice French, Rupert Hughes, and Emerson Hough (Herbert Quick and Susan Glaspell were invited but could not attend).[7] In 1917, *Prairie Gold*, described as "the first co-operative work done by Iowa writers," was published by the Iowa Press and Author's Club; in 1920, the *Palimpsest*, a monthly periodical published by the Iowa State Historical Society was founded; in 1923, Frank Luther Mott spoke before the Iowa Academy of Science and Letters in Sioux City on "Literature of Pioneer Life in Iowa" and the address was subsequently published by the State Historical Society; little magazines like the *Husk* at Cornell (1922) and the *Tanager* at Grinnell (1926) began to appear at colleges; and in 1930, *A Book of Iowa Authors by Iowa Authors* was published by the Iowa State Teachers Association.[8]

During the same period that the regionalist movement of the South (led by "fugitives" Allen Tate, John Crowe Ransom, Donald Davidson, and Robert Penn Warren) was launching its resistance to encroachment on southern agrarianism by northern industrialization, a new spirit of self-esteem manifested itself with increasing conviction in the Midwest. Among the postwar generation of writers in Iowa, there was a greater willingness both to live in the state where they were born and to use the materials of their local environment in their writing.[9] This trend was evidenced by the work of Jay G. Sigmund of Cedar Rapids, Vernon Lichtenstein at Coe College, Clarence Sundermeyer at Iowa State College at Ames, Grace Hunter at Grinnell, James Hearst of Cedar Falls, and Ruth Suckow from Hawarden, as well as Roger Sergel and Walter Muilenburg in Iowa City.[10]

Writing in 1926, Ruth Suckow declared that "the thin grasp of New England" had gradually weakened and that a native culture had begun to work its way out.[11] To substantiate the fundamental cultural change that had been "distinctly and amazingly noticeable during the last three or four years," she reported:

> A terrific rattle of typewriters has broken out. Newspapers are beginning to carry book columns of their own. People dare to send their own unsubstantiated opinions to the liberal and lively book page of the Des Moines *Register*. The group at the State university has at last been accepted as culturally respectable in spite of its native origin. The barriers have come down, to the horror of the old guard, who can really recommend no American contemporaries except Mrs. Wharton. No longer is our literature in the hands of a caste. It is snatched at by everybody—farmer boys, dentists, telegraph editors in small towns, students, undertakers, insurance agents and nobodies. All have a try at it.[12]

Five years later, a professor of English at the University of Iowa wrote of the "literary transformation" that had taken place in a single generation:

> Within our own time, we have seen the literary grip of the eastern states and the southern states loosen, and the place in fiction they once proudly held has been passed on to the Middle West—the Middle West that used to be thought of as the home of hogs and hominy, and only hogs and hominy.[13]

The author even went so far as to claim that "most of what is original in American fiction, penetrating in American fiction, and significant in American fiction the last fourteen or fifteen years has emanated from Iowa and the surrounding States."[14] As Wallace Stegner proclaimed in an article for the *Saturday Review of Literature,* the regionalists were convinced that Iowa had "definitely come of age."[15]

In sum, the literary atmosphere of Iowa City during the first decades of the twentieth century was imbued with the spirit of regionalism and charged with the special energy that emanates from sense of place and pride in locale. In addition to the stimulus of the University itself, two other factors—the *Midland* and the tradition of the writers' clubs—reflected and contributed to this spirit.

NOTES

1 Wallace Stegner, "The Trail of the Hawkeye, Literature Where the Tall Corn Grows," *Saturday Review of Literature* (July 30, 1938), 4.

2 Alice French (Octave Thanet) and Susan Glaspell were local colorists who were writing sympathetically if romantically of country life; George Cram Cook in 1903 published *Roderick Taliaferro: A Story of Maxmilian's Empire* and later founded the Provincetown Players with Susan Glaspell; Harry Hansen's later novel *Your Life Lies Before You* (1935) was set in the Davenport of this period; Arthur Davison Ficke's first two volumes of poetry were entitled *From the Isles* (1907) and *The Happy Princess* (1907); Cornelia Lynde Meigs was born just across the river in Rock Island and wrote literature for children; and Floyd Dell was at that time editing the *Tri-City Worker's Magazine,* a socialist monthly, and selling poems to *Harper's, Century,* and *McClure's.* Information from Clarence A. Andrews, *A Literary History of Iowa* (Iowa City: University of Iowa Press, 1972), pp. 26, 165ff. Andrews also cites Johnson Brigham, "Iowa's Strategic Position. A Talk with Broad-Gauge Advertisers," *Midland Monthly,* 4 (July 1895). See Andrews, pp. 242–43, for a partial list of authors published.

3 Ruth Suckow, "Iowa," *American Mercury,* 9 (1926), 43.

4 Josiah Royce, "Provincialism," *Race Questions, Provincialism, and other American Problems* (New York: Macmillan, 1908), p. 61. The text of the speech earlier appeared as a pamphlet printed for the University of Iowa by permission of the *Boston Transcript.*

5 *Ibid.,* pp. 61, 62, 98. Although Royce was careful to differentiate this "wholesome" or "higher" provincialism from narrow and disunifying "sectionalism" (which he saw as a "false form" of provincialism), and in spite of the fact that he acknowledged the value of cross fertilization of ideas and cautioned against extremes, the regionalist movement was later attacked for being narrow and xeno-

phobic. Also, in the 1930s, when the relative merits of regionalism were being debated with increasing fervor, the midwestern movement (perhaps by association with the southern agrarian movement) came to be identified with the revolt from the city—this too in contradiction to Royce's initial definition.

As Royce saw it, there were three "principal evils" to be corrected by the spirit of provincialism. The first "defect" was that the "life of our American provinces everywhere" had still "too brief a tradition." This was partly incidental, due to the newness of our country, but it was also caused by increasing geographic mobility. The second "modern evil" was an aspect of "the levelling tendency of recent civilization":

> . . . because of the ease of communication among distant places, because of the spread of popular education, and because of the consolidation and the central-ization of industries and of social authorities, we tend all over the nation, and, in some degree, even throughout the civilized world, to read the same daily news, to share the same general ideas, to submit to the same overmastering social forces, to live in the same external fashions, to discourage individuality, and to approach a dead level of harassed mediocrity.

Thirdly, provincialism would counter the psychological danger of the "mob spirit," which might erupt when social assimilation occurred too suddenly, as in moments when "the popular mind is excited" or when "great emotions affect the social order" (pp. 66, 74, 80).

Later, Allen Tate, in his call for a "return to the provinces" which were "the small self-contained centres of life," used the same terminology and approach in articu-lating the motivating ideology of the southern regionalist movement.

6 James B. Weaver, "The Authors' Homecoming of 1914," *Midland*, 1 (January 1915), 22–25. Also cited by Andrews, p. 246.

7 Andrews, p. 246.

8 *Ibid.*, pp. 248, 250, 253.

9 Stegner, 16.

10 John T. Frederick, "The Younger School," *Palimpsest*, 12 (February 1930), 78–86.

11 Suckow, 43.

12 *Ibid.*, 44.

13 Sam B. Sloan, "Misrepresentative Fiction," *Palimpsest*, 12 (February 1931), 42.

14 *Ibid.*, 43. In support of his claim, Sloan cited the following writers who be-longed "either by birth or by adoption" to the Middle West: Booth Tarkington, Willa Cather, Zona Gale, F. Scott Fitzgerald, O. E. Rolvaag, Herbert Quick, Rupert Hughes, Henry K. Webster, Sherwood Anderson, Robert Herrick, Carl Van Vechten, Josephine Herbst, Ruth Suckow, Cornelia Cannon, Sinclair Lewis, Janet Fairbank, Floyd Dell, Edna Ferber, Susan Glaspell, Margaret Ayer Barnes, and Bess Streeter Aldrich, as well as the younger novelists MacKinlay Kantor, Roger Sergel, Walter Muilenburg, and Nelson Antrim Crawford.

15 Stegner, 17.

The Regionalists

CLARKE FISHER ANSLEY was Iowa City's first important regionalist. While head of the University of Iowa's English Department from 1899 to 1917, Ansley demonstrated his interest in local culture by participating in no fewer than four writer's clubs (three of which he helped to establish) and by acting as guiding force in the founding of John T. Frederick's the *Midland* (1915-33), a magazine that became a principal exponent of the regionalist movement.

Born in Swedona, Illinois (a village within seventy miles of Iowa City), Clarke Fisher Ansley knew the Midwest and appreciated its heritage. According to his daughter, Delight, he felt a kinship with the folk element of Iowa culture:

> Not all of Father's friends were scholars. His background included farming and small towns, and he had great respect for people who could do practical work better than he could—farmers and skilled workmen. They respected him too, and they talked to him as if he were one of them.[1]

A respected Old English scholar who had done graduate work at the Universities of Leipzig, Heidelberg, and Paris, Ansley also had a deep interest in contemporary writing. He had come to Iowa City from the University of Nebraska where he had started a writing seminar for advanced students with literary ambitions. One of his students later described Clarke Ansley as a man who "was not addicted to scholarship in the usual sense." Rather, he was a man who thought of himself, and wished to be known essentially as a creative figure: "His greatest interest was in students who could show some competence and promise in creative ways." As a result, the atmosphere of the department at that time was "particularly stimulating and helpful for the young person who wanted to write."[2]

In 1917, Clarke Ansley angrily resigned from his position at the University of Iowa. The cause of his disagreement with the University is unclear. His daughter has written, "Father had a physical and mental breakdown, partly from overwork and partly from a struggle over moral principles in the affairs of the University."[3] In his book on the *Midland*, Milton Reigelman asserts that Ansley's emphasis on creative writing was being met with opposition from some administrators and faculty members. Reigelman, who credits Ansley with being "probably the first person to envision the University of Iowa as a center for creative writing," cites this conflict, along with Ansley's political stand against entry of the United States in the war, as possible causes for his resignation.[4]

After moving his family to Michigan and eventually losing his farm there, Clarke Ansley, then in his fifties, found himself jobless and deeply in debt. Following a series of editorial jobs with Macmillan, G. & C. Merriam Company, and *Encyclopaedia Britannica*, Ansley managed to recover from his misfortunes and became editor of the Columbia University Press, where he worked for eight years in preparing the first edition of the widely respected one-volume *Columbia Encyclopedia*.

In 1905, Ansley had brought to the Iowa campus Edwin Ford Piper, a former student of his who had participated in the writing seminar at Nebraska. Piper was to become one of the central figures in Iowa's developing program in creative writing. Like Ansley, he was a midwesterner who was committed to the life and culture of his locale.

Born in 1871 a few miles west of the Missouri River, Edwin Ford Piper had witnessed the farmers' encroachment on the wild and open buffalo grass country of his homeland. In this sense, Piper knew the region well. "My aim in writing has remained as constant as my subject," he once explained. "I have tried to tell the significant truth about settlement days in Nebraska." And as Ansley was well aware, Piper's approach to writing represented an exemplary application of the theory expounded by Josiah Royce:

> As I see it, in poetry, an author's subject must possess him intellectually and emotionally; he must know facts and background forgotten by everyone else, organic relations with the regional history—land—a thousand details—and then leave out all but the quintessence; he must be soaked through with the spirit originating in his subject; and his creative powers must body forth the creative and bring it to life.[5]

In addition to writing about his locale, Piper demonstrated his commitment to indigenous material by collecting folksongs, lyrics, and ballads of the West. Harry Oster, a later faculty member of the University of Iowa's English Department, described Piper's fascination with oral folklore in an article that appeared in the periodical, *Books at Iowa*:

> As a boy in Auburn, Nebraska, Piper turned an eager ear toward the folksongs of hired men, cowboys, tramps slurping their mulligan

stews from tin cans simmering over camp-fires, wandering musicians plunking their way with more gusto than profit through country fairs, horse races, and other local festivities. He also learned songs from more genteel sources: Lucinda, his mother; Ella, his sister; and the various performers, accompanying themselves on fiddle, banjo, or accordion, who entertained at meetings of the country literary society. Like many collectors, Piper started out casually, memorizing the tunes and texts he enjoyed singing to entertain his friends.[6]

Later, Piper adopted a more systematic approach, gathering song texts printed in farm journals and newspapers, transcribing ballads as they were sung to him, and purchasing the broadsides that were printed and sold at country fairs. In all, he accumulated over 1,000 items of folklore.

According to a former student, Wilma Jessea Kyvig, Edwin Ford Piper was known to his students for his "innate kindliness and gentle encouragement." She remembered him as "a superb teacher with a soft yet sonorous voice and an exceedingly quick wit."[7] But not all of his students agreed with this assessment. Another participant in Piper's creative writing seminar recalled that he and his colleagues liked Piper, but thought him too gentle, and "like most students, mocked him a little behind his back."[8] Yet another student, Ruth V. Bortin, described her experience in Piper's seminar in this way:

> As I recall his students in Creative Writing met as a group once a week, read manuscript, and criticized each other's productions. He used to tell us to keep our remarks constructive—but sometimes they were not. The atmosphere sometimes became quite heated. I remember being completely squelched on my first reading by Bob Thackaberry's remark that he considered my poems "mere twaddle." When I got several years perspective on what I was then writing I could feel amused over that, but not at the time. Piper himself was always very tactful and supportive, but he had strong ideas of what he liked. I was writing a long poem about my Grandmother, which I saw as a psychological study (not that I knew any psychology then) but he wanted me to make a tale of pioneer life in Iowa. I was so discouraged and frustrated with what I produced that I decided to switch to research for my doctoral dissertation. Personally I was fond of Prof. Piper who was a very gentle and kindly person.[9]

Because of the distinctive way in which he read his poetry aloud, many of Piper's students and friends remembered him as the "singing professor." His unique delivery was described in an article that appeared in the *Daily Iowan* at the time of his death:

Edwin Ford Piper, who came to the University of Iowa in 1905, taught courses in creative writing for thirty-four years.

John Towner Frederick, founder of the *Midland,* a magazine dedicated to promoting regional literature and pride in regional culture.

He virtually sang many of his poems; reading "Zebra Dun," he was a cowboy talking to his horse. When he said "whoa," it was not as a professor reading to class members for their souls' edification, but as a top-hand who cajoled his pinto or mustang.

When parts of a poem called for song—the lines shouted by the caller at a square dance—Professor Piper sang the lines with all the enthusiasm and gusto of the old-time caller, in time to the fiddles and "the big bass viol."[10]

As a teacher of courses in Chaucer and in poetry writing and as a leader of informal "workshop" sessions, Edwin Ford Piper was for thirty-four years a major force on the Iowa campus, a man whose relation to his students was that of a "companion who suggests rather than advises."[11]

John Towner Frederick was born on a farm in 1893 near Corning, Iowa, and came to the University of Iowa in 1909 at the age of sixteen. After two years, Frederick was forced to leave the University for financial reasons, and, from 1911 to 1913, taught in the small Adams County town of Prescott, where he became superintendent of schools and served as athletic coach and sole high school teacher. When he returned to the University in 1913, he joined and later headed Clarke Ansley's Athelney Club, a small group of students and faculty committed to learning and practicing the craft of writing.

In 1915, Frederick founded the *Midland: A Magazine of the Middle West.* In establishing the magazine, he sought to promote regional literature and a sense of regional culture. Frederick approached his task, which he saw as a challenge to the dominance of the New York based magazines and publishing houses, with all the zeal of a crusader. The magazine became a focal point for the growing regionalist movement and remained throughout the course of its eighteen-year existence a reflection of Frederick's personal hopes and convictions. From the beginning, he was warmly encouraged in his efforts by both Clarke Fisher Ansley and Edwin Ford Piper.

As Milton Reigelman points out in his book on the *Midland*, Frederick was dismayed that previous to the *Midland* there existed no general literary magazine of high quality between the Alleghenies and the Rockies. The result, as Frederick saw it, was that "young midwestern writers were more or less being forced to go East and meet publishing standards which did not allow them to treat their region realistically and honestly," and this in turn occasioned "a tendency to false emphasis, distortion, in literary interpretations." By establishing "a noncommercial magazine sympathetic to midwestern interest," Reigelman explains, Frederick hoped to encourage young writers to remain in the Midwest, which would benefit both the writers and the region.[12] Frederick expressed this notion, which was fundamental to the new journal's editorial policy, on page one of the first issue:

> Possibly the region between the mountains would gain in variety at least if it retained more of its makers of literature, music, pictures, and other expressions of civilization. And possibly civilization itself might be with us a somewhat swifter process if expression of its spirit were more frequent. Scotland is none the worse for Burns and Scott, none the worse that they did not move to London and interpret London themes for London publishers. [13]

John Towner Frederick was known as a warm, considerate man possessing a remarkable degree of patience in his work as editor of the *Midland* and in his teaching of courses in American literature and poetry writing. A frequently quoted description of Frederick was written by his colleague, Frank Luther Mott:

> Fairly tall and spare in figure, with a prominent nose on a lean and irregulary fashioned face, John Frederick was no Adonis; but there was something about him that always commanded respect. I think it was Virginia Woolf who once visited the Iowa campus and later wrote in the *Freeman* or *New Republic* a piece about Frederick that described him as "Lincolnian." That rather embarrassed him, and it was not quite right because it placed him in a heroic pose unnatural to him. Nobody on the campus was less pretentious. Kindly and sympathetic, with a ready sense of humor, Frederick maintained always a certain modest reserve of dignity. [14]

Except for brief periods of farming in Glennie, Michigan, and teaching at the University of Pittsburgh, Frederick continued to publish the *Midland* from Iowa City until 1930. At that time, he moved to Chicago to take advantage of that city's literary tradition and to make his magazine a more forceful challenge to the ascendancy of New York. It was then that Frederick changed the journal's subtitle from "A Magazine of the Middle West" to "A National Literary Magazine." By 1933, however, Frederick was forced to admit that the fourth year of the depression had been one year too many for the *Midland* and he announced the demise of the publication.

Despite the *Midland*'s increasing national scope in its last years, it never gave up its fundamentally regional and midwestern orientation. On the other hand, it is equally true that the magazine had never been totally or exclusively regional. In addition to the Iowa stories of Ruth Suckow, the Missouri sketches of Raymond Weeks, the Hoosier tales of Leo L. Ward, the Chicago pieces of James T. Farrell, the Nebraska poems of Edwin Ford

Piper and John G. Neihardt, the early works of Maxwell Anderson, Mac-Kinlay Kantor, Marquis Childs, Phil Stong, August Derleth, Albert Halper, James Hearst, and Paul Engle, contributions were also sent by William March from New York, Leonard Cline from Baltimore, Haniel Long from Pittsburgh, Howard Mumford Jones from Texas, Roland English Hartley from San Francisco, and Raymond Knister and Leyland Huckfield from Canada.[15]

In the years following the demise of the *Midland*, John Frederick continued to demonstrate his interest in young writers by publishing a number of textbooks on writing.[16] After conducting a widely popular weekly book review program called *Of Men and Books* for CBS radio in the late thirties and early forties, Frederick became head of the English Department at the University of Notre Dame, a position from which he retired in 1962, when he returned to Iowa to serve as a visiting professor until 1970.

His magazine's contribution to Iowa City—and to the State of Iowa's culture—was significant in a two-fold sense. Not only did it provide an important and respected outlet for regional authors, but it also performed the vital function of gaining for these authors national recognition—the kind of acknowledgment that inspired them with new confidence and reinforced them in their commitment to regional material. In 1930, Edward J. O'Brien (who had helped the *Midland* along in its rise to prominence by republishing a number of selected pieces in his annual collection, *Best Short Stories*) declared, "Two generations ago Boston was the geographical centre of American literary life, one generation ago New York could claim pride of place, and I trust that the idea will not seem too unfamiliar if I suggest that the geographical centre today is Iowa City."[17] Hyperbole notwithstanding, this assertion—coming as it did in the same year that an innovational program in creative writing was being formulated at the University under Norman Foerster's School of Letters—could only add to the growing conviction among resident writers that Iowa City was the place to be.

Like a number of other writers during the period of the *Midland*, Frank Luther Mott had come to the University of Iowa as a result of his interest in John Frederick's magazine, which first appeared when Mott was editing a small-town newspaper in Grand Junction, Iowa. In 1920, Mott had sent Frederick a story, "The Man With the Good Face," to consider for publication. Mott later wrote of the incident:

> Only three of my stories had been published . . . and I had a big collection of rejection slips, when I wrote the "Good Face" story. This, I felt, was something different. I sent it to a New York literary agent named Holly, with a two-dollar fee; and he replied as follows: "I regret to report that I cannot see a sale for it. . . . It has an unhealthy and

morbid theme." But John Frederick did not agree. He immediately accepted the story for the *Midland*, made a few helpful suggestions for improvements (he was always doing that for his contributors), and published it in his magazine in December, 1920. Then Edward J. O'Brien reprinted it in his *Best Short Stories* volume for 1921, and anthologies picked it up from there, and so on.[18]

Soon thereafter, when an opening developed on the Iowa faculty, it was Frederick who was instrumental in persuading Hardin Craig (chairman of the Department of English from 1919 to 1928) to hire Mott.[19] When he came to campus in 1921, Mott was already a well known figure to both the *Midland* group and the students.

Frank Luther Mott's involvement in the Iowa City literary scene was both energetic and good-natured. He played a central role in various writers' clubs, acted as an advisor to the *Iowa Literary Magazine* and the *Iowa Publisher*, and served as co-editor of the *Midland* from 1925 to 1930. In addition, he was a dedicated teacher who was not above striving to make his classes interesting and fun. One of his students later recalled:

> Mott, to lend zest to the beginning of his short-story writing course, used to offer a prize of an ice cream soda to the winner of a competition to write the best description of some campus scene. The year I took his course, we were to describe Old Capitol. I won the prize, and he was so much impressed by my description that he told me he would treat me to a lunch at the Jefferson Hotel instead of an ice cream soda. So we lunched there together in a somewhat stiff and embarrassed attempt at easy conversation. We were the only lunchers there, as I recall, in a large and gloomy dining-room. I ordered the most expensive lunch on the menu, at his urging—lake trout, which I had never eaten before. But I was so abashed (I was then a sophomore, with an Iowa farm background) that I couldn't taste what I ate. Later, on the mistaken supposition that I had a considerable literary talent which somehow needed to be released, Mott proposed to me that I get up at four o'clock every morning and simply write down whatever was in my mind. I don't know what wonderful revelations he may have expected—but I was working for my board and working for a pittance as a library page-boy, and when I got up at four there was nothing in my mind. I was simply very sleepy.[20]

Despite promising talent, Frank Luther Mott never developed as a creative writer. But as his prospects diminished in this area, he began to achieve increasing recognition for his endeavors in scholarship and journalism. In 1927, Mott was elected professor and director of the School of Journalism—succeeding Professor Charles H. Weller, who had died a few months earlier. In 1939, he was awarded a Pulitzer Prize in history for his extensive study of American magazines. During this time, Mott continued to teach courses in creative writing and in 1939, the year in which the term "Writers' Workshop" first appeared in the University *Catalogue*, he was listed as one of the five staff members.

NOTES

1   Delight Ansley, "Clarke Fisher Ansley," a pamphlet (New York: Columbia University Press, June 1974), 5.

2   Jean Wylder, an unpublished interview with John Towner Frederick, recorded October 20, 1972, at the 150-acre Paulus farm about five miles east of Iowa City. Transcript in Workshop archives.

3   Delight Ansley, *First Chronicles* (Doylestown, Penn.: Gardy Printing, 1971), p. 17.

4   Milton Reigelman, *The Midland, A Venture in Literary Regionalism* (Iowa City: University of Iowa Press, 1975), pp. 3–4.

5   Una Wallace, "A Singing Professor," *Daily Iowan* (December 6, 1931), Sunday Magazine Section, 1.

6   Harry Oster, "The Edwin Ford Piper Collection of Folksongs," *Books at Iowa*, 1 (October 1964), 28.

7   Mrs. Edward H. Kyvig, letter to the author, June 14, 1976, "Workshop Correspondence with Wilbers," no. 145, University of Iowa Archives, Iowa City.

8   Wallace Stegner, letter to John Leggett, undated, copy included in "Workshop Correspondence with Wilbers," no. 41, University of Iowa Archives, Iowa City.

9   Ruth V. Bortin, letter to the author, April 21, 1976, "Workshop Correspondence with Wilbers," no. 113, University of Iowa Archives, Iowa City.

10   Una Wallace, 1.

11   *Ibid.* In addition to his published volumes of poetry (*Barbed Wire* in 1917, *Barbed Wire and Wayfarers* in 1924, *Paintrock Road* in 1927, and *Canterbury Pilgrims* in 1935), Piper wrote a masque, entitled "The Land of the Aiouwas," which was performed on February 24 and 25, 1922, as a part of the University's Diamond Jubilee Celebration. The masque dealt with the landing of Marquette and Joliet in Iowa during their voyage down the Mississippi and its production marked the commencement of a new era of excitement and support for the creative arts at the University of Iowa. An inter-departmental effort, the masque was directed by Edward C. Mabie (then head of the Department of Speech), with music written by Philip Greeley Clapp (then head of the Department of Music).

12   Milton M. Reigelman, pp. 1–2.

13   John T. Frederick, *Midland*, 1 (January 1915), 1.

14   Frank Luther Mott, *Time Enough: Essays in Autobiography* (Chapel Hill: University of North Carolina Press, 1962), p. 126. Mott mistakenly attributes the description to Virginia Woolf, who never visited the United States.

15   Sargent Bush, Jr., "The Achievement of John T. Frederick," *Books at Iowa*, no. 14 (April 1971), 15–16; Frank Luther Mott, "The Midland," *Palimpsest,* 43 (March 1962), 140.

16   Those works included *Good Writing: A Book For College Students* (1934), *Reading for Writing: Studies in Substance and Form* (1935), which he co-edited with Leo L. Ward, *Present-Day Stories* (1941), *Out of the Midwest: A Collection of Present-Day Writing* (1944), and *American Literature: An Anthology and Critical Survey* (1949), which he co-edited with Mott and Joe Lee Davis. In his last years, Frederick published a collection of essays on nineteenth-century American novelists and religion, entitled *The Darkened Sky* (1969), a high school textbook called *Participation Texts* (1970), and a study of W. H. Hudson (1971). For more detailed information, see Sargent Bush, Jr., "The Achievement of John T. Frederick," *Books at Iowa*, 14 (April 1971), 8–30.

17   Edward J. O'Brien, *Best Short Stories of 1930* (Boston: Houghton Mifflin, 1930), p. xi. Frank Luther Mott's evocation of the spirit of place, which appeared in 1932 (in *Midland*, 19, 82–83), was reminiscent of Thoreau's observation that "the swiftest traveller is he that goes afoot" and typified the *Midland*'s editorial policy:

> There is much scurrying about the country in automobiles these days, and much accumulation of superficial ideas. The sophistication which is the goal of this kind of life is precisely the opposite of that true culture whose roots go deep into tradition and the ancient handworks and the life of the race. These things root and grow in places. There is a kind of integrity of an old man who belongs to a certain environment and nowhere else that is not found in the cosmopolite who bears a dozen veneers one imposed on another: one feels that the old man with roots is more perfect and complete. And it is because of this integrity and perfection that all the materials belonging to unspoiled places in the United States are of the highest value for painting, sculpture, poetry, fiction, and all of the more fundamental arts.

This respect for the integrity that results from long association and thorough knowledge of a particular environment was the premise at the heart of regionalism.

18   Mott, "The Midland," *Palimpsest,* 43 (March 1962), 136.

19   Reigelman, p. 22.

20   Darrell Abel, letter to the author, February 26, 1976, "Workshop Correspondence with Wilbers," no. 38, University of Iowa Archives, Iowa City.

The Writers' Clubs

IN ADDITION to the spirit of regionalism, a second element in the milieu from which the Workshop emerged was the tradition of the writers' clubs, one of the more exciting and colorful developments in Iowa City's literary history. The period of the writers' clubs began in the early 1890s and extended over the next half century. Three generations of these clubs appeared in unbroken succession and each made a unique contribution to Iowa City's literary heritage.

In order to understand the nature of the writers' clubs, it is helpful to compare them to the older literary societies from which they evolved. The first of these, the Zetagathian Society, was founded in April of 1861, less than one year after the University of Iowa began continuous operation. One of the first enduring organizations of its kind west of the Mississippi River, the Zetagathian Society remained active for some seventy years. Within three years of its founding, three more literary societies were established: the Erodelphian Society for women in October of 1862, the Hesperian Society for women in the spring of 1863, and the Irving Institute for men in February of 1864. These clubs came to dominate the literary and social life on the Iowa campus. Their purpose was to make up for an element missing in the early University curriculum. As stipulated in a historical sketch included in the 1894 yearbook, the *Hawkeye,* the founders knew "that an important and necessary element in their education was lacking—that of literary culture." It was an element that "the University did not furnish and indeed could not, owing to its limited resources."[1]

The primary activity of the literary societies was the development of rhetorical and oratorical skills. Since "literary culture" was thought to involve proficiency in public speaking, debating, and declaiming, each club emphasized these skills and took great pride in its record of debates won. In short, the literary societies concentrated on activities peripheral to the actual creation of literature. The Zetagathian Society, for one, staged public debates, organized literary programs, held weekly meetings at which literature was discussed, promoted a lecture bureau, maintained for a time its own library, and established its own newspaper.[2] In later years the Zetagathian Society, with the help of its sister society, the Hesperians, sponsored annual entertainments or "Exhibitions"—comprised of music, lectures, and debates—as well as annual plays and Memorial Day programs. From time to time, there were also special presentations like "The Old Fashioned Deestrick School," a farce that was performed June 12, 1888, in the Grand Opera House at Clinton and College streets.[3]

It was in the early 1890s, while the literary societies were still operating on a relatively strong basis, that the writers' clubs became popular in Iowa City. The Tabard was founded on "Allhalloween," 1891, and remained active for five years; Polygon was established in the spring of 1893 and lasted two decades; and Ivy Lane was organized in April of 1894 and continued operation until the early twenties. Unlike the traditional literary societies, the newer clubs were not designed merely for the study of literature or the acquisition of rhetorical skills. Like the writers' clubs found on other college campuses at the time, they were tailored for young men and women who wanted to learn and actually practice the craft of writing.

They were "writers' clubs" in the current sense of the phrase. Their purpose was to improve the participants' skills as writers by allowing each member to have a turn reading his or her original work, after which the group would respond with suggestions and literary criticism. While there was nothing particularly unique about this approach (writers have always asked friends and colleagues for feedback), the practice formalized by these clubs provided a format that could be incorporated into the classroom. Accordingly, the method (later to be called the "workshop" approach) was adopted by the University when it offered its first course in creative writing, entitled "Verse-Making Class," in the spring of 1897.

The relation between the writers' clubs and the University's Department of English was one of reciprocal influence. From the beginning, the writers' clubs had ties with the Department of English. Edward Everett Hale, Jr., head of the English Department from 1892 to 1895, was an honorary member of Polygon and George Armstrong Wauchope, his successor, was involved with the Tabard group.[4] Furthermore, a number of the student participants later joined the faculty of the English Department. George Cram Cook, who took part in the founding of the Tabard while still a student, was the man who taught the first course in poetry writing. John Gabbert Bowman, who participated as a student in both the Tabard and Ivy Lane, not only taught in the English Department, but from 1911 to 1914 served as president of the University. Similarly, Percival Hunt, who was active in Polygon, became the leading figure among the instructors of creative writing while teaching the course in short story writing from 1903 to 1921.[5] Considering the number of members common to both bodies, it is not surprising that the interests of one influenced the activities of the other.

Polygon, one of Iowa City's early "writers' clubs," was established in the spring of 1893.

This close relationship between the clubs and the University continued. When Clarke Fisher Ansley arrived on campus in 1899, he immediately became involved in Polygon. Shortly thereafter, he set up his own group called the Writers' Club and in 1905 helped establish an adjunct to the Writers' Club called the Readers' Club, which concentrated on oral presentations and interpretations of both contemporary American works as well as selections from earlier writers. Notice of an Early English Club appeared in the 1908 *Hawkeye* (the University's yearbook), but that organization was apparently short-lived.

Of longer duration and greater importance in its impact on Iowa City's literary milieu was the Athelney Club, a writers' club devoted to the study and practice of poetic art. As recorded in the diary of one member (and cited in the historical sketch prefaced to the 1918 *Athelney Book*), it was conceived on May 7, 1911, by four young men who took a walk in the country north of Iowa City "to discuss plans for forming a poets' club." Their purpose in founding the club was "to aid each other in studying and appreciating the masters of poetic art and to drill in the composition of poetry."[6] On the afternoon of May 20, according to the same source, the men had another meeting of the "poets' club" during which they spent most of their time reading their "own productions." A year later Ansley was elected an honorary member and it was he who suggested the name "Athelney," after the tiny island where King Alfred's band took refuge from the invading Danes.

Edwin Ford Piper also played an important part in the activities of Iowa City's writers' clubs. He participated in Clarke Ansley's Writers' Club and in 1909 and 1910 served as president of its adjunct, the Readers' Club. But even more important, at about the time the Athelney Club disbanded, Piper began holding outside class sessions for students interested in writing poetry. They met in Piper's basement office amidst the friendly clutter of books and papers and with the *Athelney Book* as precedent decided at the end of their fourth year to publish a collection of their poetry for local distribution. The first of four annual volumes of *Kinnikinnick* (the term refers to the mixture of sumac leaves and inner bark of a dogwood tree, smoked by the Indians and pioneers of the region) appeared in 1925. According to Pearl Minor, a former participant in these sessions, the meetings were usually attended by half a dozen or so young writers who submitted their work for oral presentation and who offered and received criticism. In an article that appeared in the March 1937 issue of *American Prefaces*, John T. Frederick recalled his involvement in these "workshop" style gatherings:

> Pictures fill my memory whenever I see or hear the name of Edwin Ford Piper—pictures that are good to hold and to turn over in the mind. I am a member of a class studying English ballads—sitting in a stiff classroom chair and listening to a reading of "Sir Patrick Spens." I carry away from the classroom not only the music and feeling of the ballad itself, but some sense and contact with the people who first made and sang it. I am a member of another class—an informal one this time: Attendance is optional, but there are few of us who fail to find our way in the late afternoon to Mr. Piper's basement office, where we sit in nooks between bookcases or even share a table with heaps of papers and magazines, and read the stories and poems and essays we have written for the comments of one another and of our leader. In that group, as rarely elsewhere in my experience, there was practiced by Mr. Piper the principle of criticism which I believe to be the only right one for dealing with student work: "Something to praise, something to blame."[7]

In the 1930s, the groups attending these sessions came to be known as the Poetry Society. Piper also was responsible for a series of "conferences for verse writers." These meetings had a more official status than the earlier gatherings in that they involved special guests and publicity, but they evolved from the same tradition. The same can be said of the "round table discussions" called "writers' workshops" which were held in Iowa City during the summer of 1939. Piper was scheduled to participate in these, but he died that spring.

Ansley's Writers' Club, the Athelney Club, and Piper's Poetry Society represent a second generation of writers' clubs in Iowa City. While modeled closely after the first generation, these clubs were unique in their new interest in publication and their emphasis on localism or regional culture. Under Ansley's and Piper's influence, these clubs encouraged their members to appreciate the value of their midwestern environment. In fact, it was from his participation in Athelney, which in 1914 began publishing annual volumes of poetry for local distribution, that John T. Frederick got the idea of establishing the *Midland*.

In terms of impact on the literary community, the third generation of Iowa City's writers' clubs reached a culmination. By popularizing the practice of inviting out-of-town writers to give public readings of their works and by injecting the literary community with a healthy dose of good-natured excitement and enthusiasm, the Saturday Luncheon Club, the Times Club, and the S.P.C.S. (Society for the Prevention of Cruelty to Speakers) made an important contribution to the atmosphere that proved so conducive to the University's developing program in creative writing.

In 1921, John Towner Frederick returned from a one-year teaching stint at the University of Pittsburgh and organized the Saturday Luncheon Club. The group held its meetings in the dining room of Youde's Inn, a huge privately owned boarding house which then stood north of the Old Capitol on Capitol Street. In organizing the endeavor, Frederick was ably assisted by Frank Luther Mott. Together, they set up an arrangement whereby each semester members would pay one dollar for each of five meetings, fifty cents of which would go for lunch and fifty cents for a guest speaker.

The Saturday Luncheon Club thus became the first writers' club to devote itself to bringing well known writers to speak on or near campus. Later described by Frederick as "the forerunner of the famous Times Club of the thirties," the club succeeded in engaging such noted authors as Carl Sandburg, Clarence Darrow, and Robert Frost, and it wasn't long before it began outdrawing the officially sponsored University lecture series. In an article that appeared in the March 1962 issue of the *Palimpsest*, Frank Luther Mott recalled:

> It is remarkable how easy it was to get the men we most wanted, and for small fees. Frederick was a persuasive fellow, and many of our notables were interested in the *Midland*. We were never able to get Henry Mencken; but we did get Sherwood Anderson and Joseph

Frank Luther Mott served as secretary-treasurer of the S.P.C.S. (Society for the Prevention of Cruelty to Speakers), Iowa City's most notorious writer's club.

Weaver and Leonard Cline and Robert Frost and Carl Sandburg and others . . . .

We spent unforgettable hours with these visitors of ours. Fixed in my memory is a picture of Frost sitting on the small of his back in an easy chair after his talk and his readings, holding a glass of milk in his hand, and regaling us between sips with amusing Amherst legends about such diverse characters as Emily Dickinson and Calvin Coolidge—wonderful stories! And Sandburg intoning folk songs to the accompaniment of his guitar. And Anderson gathered with students before a fireplace, chatting, his face in the firelight looking for all the world like that of a nice comfortable old lady. His talk, too, was mild and easy, but his ideas explosive.[8]

In spite of heated controversies caused on two occasions by the Saturday Luncheon Club, it remained active until the spring of 1929.[9] After its demise, Frank Luther Mott became involved in a Journalism Dinner Club, which continued to invite writers to lecture on a similar basis.

It was Mott's next venture, however, that succeeded in gaining the greatest fame and notoriety. With Harry Hartwick—one of the *Midland* writers—as a guiding force, Mott founded the Times Club in 1933. Following what was by this time a well established precedent, the club sold tickets in advance of the lectures. As a means of ensuring small audiences, membership was limited to three hundred people. In looking back years later, Mott marvelled at how the organizing committee "hypnotized three hundred Iowa Citians in those 'depression' years to invest two dollars apiece in an hypothetical course of this character, but the ticket sale always went over easily."[10] In fact, at the time the tickets were sold, the club did not even promise any specific program. Mott later explained:

> We told them we thought we could get five or six interesting persons to visit us—not orators or professional platform men, but persons who had done things, and had ideas, and were willing to talk informally to a small audience of intelligent and sympathetic listeners. Watch the papers, we said, and you will see who they are and when they are to be here; that will be your sole notification of the meetings.[11]

Mott cited two reasons for the club's success in bringing writers to speak: Iowa City's proximity to Chicago, which made it possible for eastern writers visiting that metropolis to include a side-trip to Iowa City, and the Times Club's growing reputation. Among the club's guests were the novelist O. E. Rolvaag (author of the classic, *Giants in the Earth*), Henry A. Wallace (who later became vice-president under Franklin Roosevelt), Donald R. Murphy (editor of *Wallace's Farmer*), Lincoln Steffens (the muckraking editor of *McClure's*), and Christopher Morley (the New York critic and author whose novels included *Parnassus on Wheels* and *Kitty Foyle*). In addition, the Times Club also brought Frost and Sandburg once again to Iowa City.

The Times Club gave birth to one of the more spirited and fun-loving groups in Iowa City's literary history. While Grant Wood, Iowa's regionalist painter, was commuting from Cedar Rapids twice a week to lecture at the University and was lunching with Mott every Tuesday at "Smitty's" Cafe on Dubuque Street, the executive committee of the Times Club was being enlarged to sixteen members. This inner group, of which Grant Wood became a member, was dubbed by Mott as "The Society for the

Prevention of Cruelty to Speakers." Though the first president of the S.P.C.S. was Evans A. Worthley and the first vice-president Jeanne Doran, the "three wheel-horses of the organization," according to Mott, were Grant Wood, Clyde Hart, and Mott himself, the "eager beaver" secretary-treasurer. Membership was kept near sixteen and was divided among faculty, students, and townspeople. [12]

The chief function of this whimsical group was to spare guests of the Times Club undue harassment from overly zealous civic groups and individuals. Its members planned to accomplish this by entertaining the guest writers at after-lecture parties given in their honor. For this purpose, the group decided that they needed a place with the right atmosphere. They considered various possibilities, including an abandoned country schoolhouse, a barn, and an old flour mill, but they were unable to agree until Roland Smith (known otherwise as "Smitty") offered them, rent free, the entire floor above his cafe. Given carte blanche, the members outdid themselves in furnishing and decorating the space, using it as two rooms—a dining room and a parlor—in what Grant Wood "affectionately" called "the worst style of the late Victorian period."[13]

Each member of the group was permitted to invite two guests and according to Mott the rooms were always filled. Mott himself would occasionally provide the evening's entertainment with his passionately melodramatic reading of "The Face on the Bar Room Floor." Sometimes Sigmund Spaeth would play the organ and "Steamboat Bill" Petersen (later superintendent of the State Historical Society of Iowa) would lead the group in old comic German songs. At a party given for MacKinlay Kantor, the guest of honor reportedly proffered a fervent recitation of "The Rebel's Prayer." Other guests included Thomas Hart Benton, Stephen Vincent Benét, John Erskine, Gilbert Seldes, Nicholas Roosevelt, Edward J. O'Brien, Thomas A. Craven, Frederick Essary, Bruce Bairnsfather, Sterling North, John G. Neihardt, Thomas W. Duncan, Elmer Peterson, Lewis Worthington Smith, and Alfred M. Bailey, all of whom posed derisively with false beards and moustaches for photographs later displayed in a red plush album. In addition, the society invited and entertained a number of blacks, including W. C. Handy, composer of "The St. Louis Blues"; Rosamund Johnson, a musician who accompanied and aided the near blind Handy; Rosamund's brother, James Weldon Johnson, who was then known as the "dean" of Negro poets; and poets Countee Cullen and Langston Hughes. [14]

Ironically—or perhaps appropriately for a group of its nature—the guest who generated the most publicity was the guest who never came. The incident, which came to be known as "the Stein fiasco," occurred on December 10, 1934, when an enthusiastic audience assembled and eagerly awaited Gertrude Stein.

When the S.P.C.S. learned that Gertrude Stein and Alice B. Toklas were planning a visit to the United States and that Stein was planning to lecture at Columbia and the University of Chicago, it immediately set about trying to coax her to come to Iowa City. With the helpful suggestions of Rousseau Vorhies, an acquaintance of both Mott's and Stein's, the club tried a variety of approaches, including the ruse of organizing a "Rose Is A Rose Club," having the members photographed wearing white roses at a special dinner (the organization's one and only meeting), and sending the picture of the dinner party to Gertrude Stein. Mott later wrote of his efforts to satisfy her conditions for coming:

> She yielded to our blandishments and consented to come to us, for a very reasonable fee. . . . But by the time she had reached New York she had quarreled violently with Rousseau, and wired me to know if we had any connection with him. When I reassured her on that point, she wired me again to know if we were keeping the audience small. When I told her we always kept our audiences small, she sent me another telegram to find out how small. Between us, we kept Western Union busy for a day or two; but she finally said all right, she was coming, and she would speak on "The Making of *The Making of Americans*."[15]

The *Daily Iowan's* front-page headline for September 14 read, "GERTRUDE STEIN TO LECTURE HERE," and the Times Club was inundated with requests for tickets. In spite of all the carefully laid plans, however, the club's moment of greatest glory was foiled by a sudden winter storm. Mott reported:

> Came the tenth of December, and one of those great sleet storms which Iowa sometimes suffers. But our audience braved it all, some driving more than a hundred miles over icy roads. The audience was there, all of it, with perhaps a few more than the stipulated number; but the Misses Stein and Toklas, who had been scheduled to arrive by special plane in the early evening, were not there. About eight-thirty a Western Union boy arrived at our crowded lecture hall with the last of the series of telegrams from Miss Stein. It read: "PLANE GROUNDED WAUKESHA, WISCONSIN, GERTRUDE STEIN."[16]

The Times Club and its spirited auxiliary, the Society for the Prevention of Cruelty to Speakers, disbanded because, in a sense, they were too successful. According to Mott, the University Lecture Committee apparently resented the way the unofficial clubs seemed always able to grab the headlines. Eventually Mott was called into a conference with the president of the University and the chairman of the Lecture Committee, at which time he agreed to suspend operation of the Times Club after a year's moratorium. Some of its members thought that he had given in too easily and Mott himself later came to agree that he probably had.

From the days of the Zetagathian Society to those of the Tabard in the 1890s and the Times Club in the 1930s, a certain excitement and spirit of place took shape and came to fruition in Iowa City. With the appearance of each generation of clubs, that spirit was renewed and revitalized. Each made a unique contribution to Iowa City's literary heritage and had a direct bearing on the course of events within the University structure. Before the University was able to do its share in providing students with a "literary culture," there were the literary societies; before there were "workshop" classes, there were informal "workshop" gatherings; and before the English Department and later the Writers' Workshop began sponsoring regular lectures and readings by guest writers, there were clubs like the Saturday Luncheon Club, the Times Club, and the memorable S.P.C.S.

On the other hand, one should take care not to overestimate the importance of regionalism or the writers' clubs. To suggest that the Writers' Workshop was a product of the *Midland*'s influence or that it evolved from the writers' clubs would be wrong. Without the determined efforts of men like Norman Foerster, it is unlikely that the University of Iowa would have sponsored the nation's first full-fledged program in creative writing. Furthermore, neither regionalism nor the writers' clubs and their predecessors, the literary societies, were unique to Iowa City. Regionalism was a movement of national scope, and during the nineteenth and early twentieth centuries literary organizations were common on college campuses. But it is undeniable that regionalism and the writers' clubs in Iowa City were significant factors in the Workshop's emergence, for together they created an atmosphere that was vibrant with interest in creative writing.

NOTES

1   1894 *Hawkeye* (Iowa City), p. 90.

2   *Vidette*, which first appeared in October of 1879, and the school newspaper, *University Reporter*, consolidated in September 1881 to become *Vidette-Reporter*. In the autumn of 1901, *Vidette-Reporter* and the *S.U.I. Quill*, which had been published since 1891, combined to form the *Daily Iowan*, which was first issued September 21, 1901. Information from 1932 *Hawkeye* (Iowa City), p. 28.

3   Theodore Wanerus, *The History of The Zetagathian Society* (Iowa City: The Zetagathian Society, 1911). The Grand Opera House occupied the second and third floors of the present First Federal Building at Clinton and College streets. Location of this and other historic sites from Irving Weber's *Iowa City* (Iowa City: Iowa City Lions Club, 1976).

By the turn of the century, however, the influence of the four original organizations had begun to diminish. Because of competition from newly founded societies and fraternal orders, because of an increase in faculty control over student affairs, and because of a more replete curriculum, they became less of a force in campus life. While it was not uncommon for the Zetagathian Society in its first decades to attract as many as two hundred visitors to a program, by 1911 visitors were rare, except during the first few weeks of school. Notwithstanding their diminished stature, all four societies continued operations throughout the twenties, when there was a brief resurgence of literary societies with the establishment of the Hamlin Garland, Whitby, and Athena societies for women.

These organizations are best characterized as "study groups." The Hamlin Garland Society, for instance, devoted itself to the study of Garland's works and even played a part in bringing him to campus. The following excerpt from *Hamlin Garland's Diaries* (Donald Pizer, ed., San Marino: Huntington Library, 1968, p. 264) is dated April 25, 1927, and contains Garland's impression of the students and the town:

> At three I spoke to about one hundred students in a small amphi-theater in the science building, talking informally of Howells, Clemens, Riley, Eggleston, and Burroughs. At four my young people came and took a little turn about the place. At eight we faced an audience of nearly two thousand people in the auditorium and pleased them mightily with our "show." It was a fine audience with many young people in it. They liked Mary Isabel and Hardesty and applauded them heartily.
>
> The general effect of Iowa City is heartening. It is American, although it is evident that the literary "radicalism" of Mencken and his crowd is largely followed. There are certain of the professors who worship at the Mencken-Wellsian shrine and instill in their pupils a cynical disregard of "the nineties." To all I said they listened respectfully but no doubt held to all their radical notions. They all want to write. They all hear of fortunes being made in authorship and so they are for it.

4   Edward Everett Hale, Jr., was the son of the New England orator.

5   Interestingly, Iowa City's first generation of writers' clubs shared many characteristics with the social fraternities, which were then becoming increasingly popular. Prospective members of both sexes were "rushed" at dinners and parties. The clubs had distinguishing pins, emblems, mottoes, colors, and even yells. For instance, Ivy Lane's colors were ivy green and pearl grey, while Polygon's yell went like this:

Wa Hoo! Wa Hoo!
On! On! On!
We are, We are!
Poly, Polygon!

Information relating to these clubs is based on descriptions appearing in various issues of the *Hawkeye*.

6 Ivan McPeak, "Historical, 1913–1918," *Athelney Book*, 5 (1918), 7.

7 John T. Frederick, "A Maker of Songs," *American Prefaces*, 2 (March 1937), 83.

8 Frank Luther Mott, "The S.P.C.S.," *Palimpsest*, 43 (March 1962), 117. This material also appears in *Time Enough: Essays in Autobiography* (Chapel Hill: University of North Carolina Press, 1962), pp. 132–45.

9 The first episode occurred in 1925, when John Frederick extended the invitation to Sherwood Anderson. According to the account in Milton Reigelman's book, certain townspeople, upon seeing Anderson's books in the local bookstores and learning that he was coming to lecture, demanded the lecture be cancelled to prevent Sherwood Anderson from "planting seeds of sexual revolution in Iowa City." Pressure was exerted on the University President, Walter Jessup, to fire Frederick should he persist in his plans to bring Anderson to town. Frederick, however, refused to cancel the lecture and he was backed in his decision by Hardin Craig, then head of the Department of English. Anderson did come and speak as scheduled, but after so much prior debate the relative mildness of his remarks seemed anticlimactic. (Reigelman narrates the whole episode in *The Midland*, p. 18.)
The second incident occurred four years later when the Saturday Luncheon Club experienced unfavorable publicity because of the unexpected remarks of a supposedly non-controversial figure. John V. A. Weaver, born in North Carolina and best known for his poetry—though also known as a New York critic, Hollywood screen writer, novelist, and playwright—ventured some criticisms of prohibition while lecturing in Iowa City. His remarks angered a group of citizens from Oelwein, Iowa, and they sent letters of protest to the *Des Moines Register* and to the university's Office of the President. The brouhaha gradually died down, but not before Frank Luther Mott felt compelled to send a letter defending the club to President Jessup. At the end of that letter, Mott noted that the Saturday Luncheon Club would probably suspend activities in May of 1929 because it had not been financially successful in the last year or so. (Frank Luther Mott, letter to Marcella Hotz, Office of the President, August 3, 1929, copy in "Frank Luther Mott," University of Iowa Archives, Iowa City, Iowa.)

10 Mott, "The S.P.C.S.," 118.

11 *Ibid.*

12 *Ibid.*, 125–26. Evans A. Worthley was pastor of the Unitarian Church and Clyde Hart a prominent attorney in Iowa City.

13 *Ibid.*, 122, 124. Mott re-created the scene with this description:

> We put an ingrain carpet on the floor and a flowered paper on the walls. We decorated with Currier and Ives prints; a fine chromo of that old favorite, "Rock of Ages," in which a lady clings to the foot of a cross on a great rock lashed by foam-tipped waves from the sea; embroidered mottoes, "God Bless Our Home," "Peace Be With You," and so on; and certain designs under glass formed from the hair of some dear departed. In the dining-room section a big table was covered with a red-and-white checked cloth, and a bulging sideboard stood in one corner. In the parlor, was much red plush and walnut furniture—Boston rockers, and love-seats on either side of the marble fireplace. One big chair was made of steers' horns, with seat, back, and tassels of green plush. A cottage organ, with elaborately carved walnut case and music

rack, was ornamental, and proved highly useful at our parties. Upon a marble-topped stand stood a red-plush album, which, in the course of time, came to be filled with specially posed pictures of our guests and our own members. . . . Almost always, conversation began with our guests' exclamations about the furnishings of our rooms. "Oh, my aunt had a decoration piece of peacock feathers just like that in her front parlor! And it was set on just such a marble-topped stand!" We came to expect, and to await with pleasure such an upsurge of nostalgic memories on the part of every middle-aged visitor who saw our exhibition for the first time.

14 The group also prepared a flier, which Mott described as "a whimsical invitation to come and visit . . ., address the Times Club, and see if the Society for the Prevention of Cruelty to Speakers lived up to its name. This carried a charming decoration in the style of the Nineties showing a hand pouring water from a rose-decorated pitcher into a hobnail-glass tumbler. Grant Wood made the original as a pen-and-ink drawing and we reproduced it on the cover of our brochure" (Mott, 126–27). The flier read as follows:

Dear Friend and Prospective Guest:
   As we look forward to your coming to us on   , we are hoping that it may prove to be a happy visit for you. We wish to do all that we can to make it so. To that end, would you be good enough to jot down some memoranda here:
   Do you wish us to make hotel reservations?
   Or, do you wish to be entertained at a private home?
   Do you wish to be met at the train?   If so, when do you expect to arrive?
   Do you wish to meet a small group of "kindred spirits" informally? The Executive Committee of the Club would be delighted to give a small luncheon or dinner for you while you are here, but we do not wish to impose upon your good nature. Please let us know your wish in the matter.
   Do you wish to Rotarianize, Kiwanisize, Lionize, or otherwise yield to the importunities of service clubs or similar groups while in our midst? We're just asking you.
   Have you any suggestions as to the introduction before your lecture?
   Is there any other way in which we can serve you?
   We look forward with the pleasantest anticipation to your visit. [p. 129]

15 Mott, "The S.P.C.S.," 130–31.

16 *Ibid.*, 131.

II

EMERGENCE

The Early Program in Creative Writing

THE FIRST course in "imaginative" or "creative" writing at Iowa was listed in the University *Catalogue* of 1895–96 and taught in the spring of 1897. "Verse-Making Class" was one of fourteen offered that year by the Department of English. Its description in the catalogue read as follows:

> Practice in metrical composition in the fixed forms of verse such as the heroic couplet, Spenserian stanza, ode, rondeau, sonnet, ballad, and song. Analysis of the best examples of these forms in English poetry. Informal discussions of artistic questions.[1]

Though perhaps more prescriptive than later courses in creative writing, "Verse-Making Class" possessed the elements of the basic "workshop" gathering: writing by the participants, criticism, and general discussion of "artistic questions."

The instructor, George Cram Cook of Davenport—or "Jig" as he was known to his friends—shared rooms with another young teacher. According to Susan Glaspell, the two were considered "a little wild." In her biography, *The Road to the Temple*, she wrote, "You sat by an open fire, and were given rum in your tea when you came to see them. There were Chinese hangings. Iowa City was not quite sure. Brilliant—yes; but sometimes they looked as if they had been drinking the night before."[2] Moreover, there were stories of Jig playing the violin for his students during class and of wild horseback riding at night.

Loquacious, energetic, and unmistakably offbeat, George Cram Cook was as inspirational in the classroom as he was domineering. Though possessed by a "passion for education," he was known also for his "hearty instinct against authority." Susan Glaspell described and illustrated his attitude in this way:

> He never reported an absence. If his students were interested they would come. If they weren't interested, why should they come? He would really rather they didn't. But they did come, wanting to see what charming truancy their teacher would next devise and gravely lead them to.

There was a girl who persistently forgot examinations, so he finally sent her an invitation:

Mr. George Cram Cook
Requests the pleasure of
Miss May Morris Company
In Jackson Hall
Friday, at eleven
Examination

And in examination Miss Morris might be asked: "Have you felt anything in Dante's poetry which relates it to life in Iowa City?"[3]

When war was declared against Spain in April of 1898, George Cook quit teaching and joined the Iowa Volunteer Infantry. Following periods of gathering material in Mexico for a novel, truck farming in Davenport, and writing for Floyd Dell and the *Friday Literary Review* of the *Chicago Evening Post*, George Cook founded, in 1916 (with Susan Glaspell), the Provincetown Players and directed and sustained that experimental group for six years.[4] In 1922, he and Susan Glaspell sailed for Greece, where he lived the last two years of his life, donning the traditional shepherd's garb and becoming a local legend at his death.

"Verse-Making Class" was offered again the next year, but under a new title, "Versification." After George Cram Cook left Iowa, Sam Berkley Sloan took over the course under a third title, "Poetics." And when the first course in short story writing appeared in the 1900–01 University *Catalogue*, Sam Sloan was listed as the instructor. "The Short Story" was described as a "course in narrative and descriptive prose and the art of modern prose fiction, the short story being the form selected for practice" and admission was "by consent of the instructor."[5] The next year the course was given a sequential format, with the first semester devoted to study and the second to practice. The two descriptions were:

> Studies in descriptive and narrative prose, and in the structure of the short story. Typical stories by Poe, Hawthorne, and their successors are considered in detail.

> Practice in descriptive and narrative writing, the short story being the form selected. Criticism by students and instructor.[6]

Unlike the early course in poetry writing, American authors were being used as models in the short story course—at a time when courses in American literature were uncommon at most universities. Both courses relied on the "workshop" method of offering material for group criticism.

Although the poetry and short story writing courses were soon taken over by other instructors, Sam Sloan continued to teach courses in the essay, advanced composition, and American and English novel until his retirement in 1939. In the course of his long career, Sloan was enormously popular with his students, who remembered him for the heated lectures in which he ripped his dark rimmed spectacles from his face "a hundred times an hour," pounded the desk furiously, pressed his fists into his forehead, and swooped "across the blackboard leaving a trail of mysterious crosses and asterisks behind him."[7] When interviewed by the *Daily Iowan* in 1948, Sloan recalled his early days at the University:

> "When I first came here," Sloan reminisced, "the equipment of the university was very meagre. It was housed in old brick buildings which have since burned down, fortunately, perhaps.
>
> "And yet," he mused, "it was so great in teachers—men like Currier, Calvin, Nutting, McBride [sic], Ansley, Patrick and Seashore, who fairly exuded personality in and out of the classroom."
>
> There were advantages to the small enrollment of those days, he noted.
>
> "When I was teaching freshman and sophomore classes in the university, I knew personally almost every student in the liberal arts college. It was easy, because there were only about 600 in the college at that time, and I'd had most of them in classes."[8]

Sam Sloan lived the rest of his days in Iowa City. Every year former students would stop and see him on their visits to campus. When he became too feeble to leave his room on the seventh floor of the Jefferson Hotel, he occupied himself by reading and watching from his perch the movement and life of the city below him. Sloan died on May 1, 1967, at the age of ninety-two.

Like George Cook and Sam Sloan, Percival Hunt was both student and teacher at Iowa. After graduating with a B.A. in 1902, Percival Hunt was for two decades the leading figure among the instructors of creative writing. He first taught "The Short Story" in 1903 and, with the exception of the academic year 1907–08, continued to do so until 1921, when he resigned and the course was taken over by Frank Luther Mott. During his tenure, it was assumed that any student who was seriously interested in learning to write would study under Hunt.

As an instructor, Percival Hunt was a natural, a teacher *par excellence.* His approach was personal in the sense that he stressed the importance of his students' individuality and personalities. He insisted that they reveal and invest a part of their true selves in his course, that they make everything they wrote a genuine expression of themselves. "A good teacher," he asserted, "needs more than ideas. He needs feeling about these ideas and about his students. He needs to realize the humanity of those he teaches; they, like him, are more than holders of facts."[9]

In the 1920s, the three principal figures in the teaching of creative writing at Iowa were Edwin Ford Piper, John Towner Frederick, and Frank Luther Mott. Like Sloan, Hunt, and Ansley, none of these instructors achieved national recognition as a writer, but their various activities in support of the creation of literature constituted the mainstay of the University's developing program in creative writing. Edwin Ford Piper took over the course in poetry writing from John Gabbert Bowman, who had taught it for two years after Sam Sloan had relinquished the position.[10] Piper taught the class in alternate years until 1918 and then every year until 1939.

During this period of high literary interest, John Towner Frederick's and Frank Luther Mott's courses in short story writing and American literature attracted 100 or more students each semester. Students also took advantage of a new advanced short story writing course, designed for those who were interested in further study of the form. The chief difference between the format of these early classes and that of the later Workshop courses was that in the early classes the student writing was not duplicated and distributed in advance, but was read aloud—usually by the author—during the class session. Even when copies were made in advance, the short stories were presented orally. As John Frederick later explained, the work "was read aloud even though they [the students] had the multigraphed copy in their hands, because I've always held that the oral interpretation was a significant part of the impression—the total impression—of a work of fiction."[11] Following the oral presentation of the story, the group would then offer comments and criticism, although in Frank Luther Mott's classes there was, purportedly, more lecture than real discussion.

The 1920s were a time of thriving activity, not only in the area of imaginative writing, but in various creative arts at the University of Iowa. In addition to the developing program in imaginative writing—to say nothing of the highly respected program in expository writing under the direction of Carrie Stanley—important strides were being made in several departments. The Theater Department, under the direction of E. C. Mabie, was attaining national prominence, while the first course devoted solely to playwrighting (taught by Leigh Sowers) appeared in the 1923–24 University *Catalogue*. In music, Philip Greeley Clapp, who had become head of the department in 1919, founded the University of Iowa Symphony Orchestra in 1921 and under his direction Iowa later became one of the first schools to offer the Ph.D. in musical composition. Yet another indication of the progressive attitude then prevalent at Iowa was the founding in 1927 of the School of Religion, which stands as the nation's first department of religious studies in a tax-supported college.

The man who was in large part responsible for this climate was Carl Seashore, who had become dean of the Graduate College in 1908, after having served as professor of philosophy, professor of psychology, and head of the Psychology Department. Author of *Psychology of Music* (1938), Carl Seashore led the University into taking the innovational step of accepting creative work—in addition to scholarly research—for advanced degrees in the arts. In the 1922–23 University *Catalogue,* there appeared for the first time the following statement under the heading, "Master of Arts and Master of Science":

> The candidate shall submit a thesis showing independent scholarship and marked creative attainment in some branch of learning. . . . The thesis requirement may be interpreted broadly so as to include artistic production, the performance of a project, or the intensive study of a special topic. [12]

This arrangement not only made the University of Iowa one of the first institutions in the country to accredit creative work for advanced degrees in all the arts, but later, when the option was extended to the requirements for a Ph.D., it also served to distinguish Iowa's creative writing program from any other program in the country.

Though instituted in 1922, no one took advantage of the new arrangement until 1925, when Marian E. Edman and Anna M. Starbuck received the first creative masters' degrees from the Department of Music for their original symphonic compositions. The next year, the Department of Art granted a Master of Arts degree to Alma M. Held for her painting, "Representation." In the Department of English, Josephine Donovan wrote a novel, *Black Soil,* originally to be used as her master's thesis in 1929, but when she won a $2,000 prize for the work, she decided not to submit it as a thesis. Another woman, Mary Hoover Roberts, was the first person to receive a Master of Arts degree from the English Department under the new arrangement when her collection of poems, *Paisley Shawl,* was accepted in 1931. In the following year, the English Department awarded five creative masters' degrees, including those of Wallace Stegner and Paul Engle. When Engle's thesis, *One Slim Feather,* appeared under the new title, *Worn Earth,* it became the University's first thesis of poems to be published.

Even as the program became more firmly established, the emphasis of the English Department seemed to be shifting away from the area of imaginative writing. Upon the occasion of Hardin Craig's resignation as head of the department in 1928, John T. Frederick wrote to University President Walter Jessup:

> The selection of Mr. Craig's successor will, it seems to me, involve a rather definite choice, as to the future policy of our English depart-

ment, between increased service to the literary development of the state and of the region, on the one hand, and increased contribution to the general cause of academic research on the other.

I know that you are fully aware of the many evidences of a rapidly awakening literary consciousness in Iowa and in the other states of the middle west. Chiefly because of the foundations laid by Professor Ansley and Professor Hunt, and in some degree because of the work of Professor Piper, Professor Mott, and myself, the University of Iowa is in a position of acknowledged leadership in this development. I believe that the people of the state recognize and value this achievement of the University.

In recent years, however, the tendency in our English department has been toward increased emphasis upon philological investigation. It dominates our graduate work to the almost complete exclusion of creative effort. The natural effect is to fill the ranks of our instructors with men and women whose primary interests are in research, and this interest is of course expressed in their teaching. Within a few years, by the continuation of this process, our leadership in creative effort in our region will be lost.

Frederick went on to point out that his plea should not be interpreted as a personal complaint against Hardin Craig, who had been "uniformly kind and helpful" toward him. He concluded:

I believe that in the one direction lies unique distinction for our university, and a positive service to our state and region which our people will not be slow to appreciate. In the other direction lies an achievement perhaps intrinsically valuable, but lacking in immediate interest and worth to the people of the state of Iowa, and one in which we cannot hope, for many years at least, to rival the older and richer universities with which, in the field of research, we come into competition. [13]

Although Frederick had recommended Piper to replace Craig—and Mott had recommended Frederick—a third man, Baldwin Maxwell, was appointed. [14] While Maxwell was not unsympathetic to the expanding Program in Creative Writing, neither was he the man finally responsible for leading the University in what Frederick considered the direction of "unique distinction." That the University did achieve this distinction is owing rather to the efforts of Norman Foerster and those who followed him.

_____

NOTES

1   1895–96 *University of Iowa Catalogue*, p. 38.

2   Susan Glaspell, *The Road to the Temple* (New York: Frederick A. Stokes, 1927), p. 86.

3   *Ibid.*, p. 82. According to Glaspell, George Cook both loved and hated his native State of Iowa. As a student, he had been inspired by the teaching of Melville B. Anderson (then head of the English Department), whom he later referred to as "the man who first awoke in me the love of letters and thereby shaped my life." Moreover, the University library had been the scene of a compelling vision, in which Cook claimed to have perceived suddenly the unity of himself with the universe and to have had instilled in him an ever-abiding yearning for beauty. He sensed a communion between Athens and Iowa City, with the classic Greek architecture of the latter's centerpiece, the Old Capitol building, and he once observed that the two cities shared "the mystery of existence deeply." He was also capable of writing sympathetically of the Iowa environment, once describing the sluggish Iowa River as "that strange little wooded river valley, which has not yet lost its Indian character" (*Ibid.*, p. 80).

On the other hand, George Cook felt oppressed by what he considered his generally unattractive and dismal surroundings and by the undramatic nature of small-town existence. He thought the system of education at the University to be dull, lifeless, and stifling. About those he taught, he wrote: "Students poor. They come from farmers and retail tradespeople, children of lawyers, physicians, in country towns. They come determined to make their education 'practical'—that is, worth money. Puritanic distrust of pleasure and beauty" (*Ibid.*).

In his description of the town of Iowa City as it was just before the turn of the century (in which he inaccurately described the area as "flat"), George Cook seemed to link the effects of an oppressive cultural or religious influence to the physical environment:

> The town stood among vast pastures and cornfields fenced with barbed wire. Looking from the tower of the college building the monotony of flat plain was broken only by the willows which lined a sluggish river, and by an occasional row of poplars, planted to protect some barren farmhouse from the winds. In the town the wide streets were always either muddy or dusty, ashes and refuse were dumped by the wooden sidewalks. The low brick business buildings came to have a repugnant vitality, suggesting lines of dwarfed and dirty soldiers. [There was] one avenue of green yards, elms and maples, good frame-houses of the colonial type. The older men talked shop; the women, babies and cake. The younger men were unattractively pious or unattractively wicked. A dismal Puritanism waged war with a dismal vice. Hardly any one seemed to grow up there; and there was from the cradle to tombstone something inherently undramatic in their lives. [*Ibid.*, p. 80.]

4   G. Thomas Tanselle, "George Cram Cook and the Poetry of Living, with a Checklist," *Books at Iowa*, 24 (April 1976), 5.

5   1900–01 *University of Iowa Catalogue*, p. 98.

6   1901–02 *University of Iowa Catalogue*, p. 112.

7   Louis Cook, Jr., "Sam Sloan, Teacher Extraordinary, Retires to His Flowers," *Des Moines Register* (April 30, 1939).

8   Ardath Youmans, "Professor Sloan Recalls Days at S.U.I.," *Daily Iowan* (May 20, 1948).

9   Percival Hunt, *If by Your Art, Testament to Percival Hunt* (Pittsburgh: University of Pittsburgh Press, 1948), p. xiii.

Unlike Cook, Sloan, and Hunt, Clarke Fisher Ansley never taught a course in creative writing at the University of Iowa. However, as head of the English Department from 1899 to 1917, his interest in creative writing was reflected in the curriculum. In the 1916–17 University *Catalogue,* the category of courses in composition and exposition for undergraduates was expanded to include a course entitled, "Description and Narration," which was offered continuously—though with some modification—until 1939. The course was first taught by Mary Grove Chawner, who had been with the department since 1904 and who had been active in Ansley's Writers' Club. During Hardin Craig's term as chairman, the study of narrative writing as a creative art was continued and Walter John Muilenburg's course, "Introduction to Narrative Writing," was offered as a supplement to the original course.

10   John Gabbert Bowman served as chancellor of the University from 1911 to 1914, when he resigned because of a dispute over jurisdiction with the Board of Education. Accepting a position at the University of Pittsburgh, he became known as the man responsible for the construction of Pittsburgh's Cathedral of Learning.

11   Jean Wylder, unpublished interview with Frederick, recorded October 20, 1972. Transcript in University of Iowa Archives, Iowa City.

12   1922-23 *University of Iowa Catalogue,* p. 84.

13   John T. Frederick, letter to President Walter Jessup, January 28, 1928, Presidents' Correspondence 1927–28, folder no. 40, University of Iowa Archives, Iowa City.

14   Reigelman, *The Midland, A Venture in Literary Regionalism* (Iowa City: University of Iowa Press, 1975), p. 32.

New Humanism, Regionalism, and the Imagination

THE WRITERS' WORKSHOP emerged as a full-fledged program during a period of disparate influences. During the 1930s and early 1940s, Norman Foerster sought to give the Iowa Program in Creative Writing a broader, non-regionalist orientation. Yet at the same time the regionalist spirit of the 1920s not only continued to manifest itself, but became increasingly partisan in tone. The result was a curious equilibrium of forces. There existed in Iowa City a peculiar balance between new humanist concerns and regionalist pride, an interplay between the voices of change and the impetus of tradition. It was in the unique environment created by the confluence of these currents that the Writers' Workshop came into being.

Norman Foerster came to Iowa from the University of North Carolina. He was hired to serve as director of the newly formed School of Letters, which had been established at the prompting of Dean George F. Kay for the purpose of unifying the four language departments (English, German, Latin and Greek, and Romance) and breaking down "the barriers" which had hindered "the proper coordination and integration of studies in language and literature."[1]

In the summer of 1930, steps were taken to sponsor imaginative writing as a discipline in Iowa's graduate school. Foerster explained later in a letter to John Gerber (who in 1961 became head of the Department of English): "I wrote out my four-fold program, one of which as you know gave full recognition to imaginative writing for both graduate degrees." He could recall "no expression of dissent" when he sent the program to the full professors of the department for suggestions, but he suspected that "virtually all of them were embarrassed."[2] While this was hardly the case, Frank Luther Mott (who himself "heartily and even enthusiastically" supported the program) confided at the time to President Jessup that he "should be greatly surprised if Professor Foerster's plan should go through the graduate faculty without opposition."[3] Later, when the plan was formally presented to the faculty, there was—according to Foerster's recollection—"negligible if any discussion." He wrote: "The vote was taken, and there was no audible 'no.' I assumed that there was large dissent, but that it was not voiced because no one quite knew what to do about the new office and hesitated to begin by opposing."[4]

Early in 1931, Norman Foerster made the dramatic announcement that a new field for graduate study had been opened by the School of Letters. On March 26, an article explaining the new program appeared in the *Daily Iowan* under the heading "Iowa's School of Letters Admits Imaginative, Critical Writing for Ph.D. Thesis." The article read in part:

> In published announcements of recent years, the graduate college has defined the scope of creative scholarship in such a way as to permit the substitution of a poem, play, or other work of art for the more usual type of dissertation.
>
> In accordance with this provision, Professor Foerster said, the school of letters is working out a type of discipline suitable for candidates whose literary interests are of a sort not at present given recognition in American graduate schools.
>
> Today, he explained, the dissertation is everywhere viewed as a piece of research in language or in literary history, these two fields being conceived as a means of understanding literature. The school of letters, however, believes that there are two other means of understanding literature, by creating it and by criticizing it.
>
> All candidates for the Ph.D. will be expected to form some acquaintance with all four of these means. They may specialize in any one, language, literary history, literary criticism, or imaginative writing.[5]

Foerster went on to emphasize that the School of Letters did not propose "to establish a vocational school for authors and critics"—though this is what the program soon came to resemble as it evolved into the Writers' Workshop—but that the innovation was intended rather as a needed addition to a larger discipline. That discipline was literary research in its broadest sense, which Foerster described as "the endeavor of an independent mind to render clearer some part of human experience through any form of literary activity." The proper role of criticism, as opposed to the treatment of literature "as if it were a branch of science," was then alluded to in much the same terms that Foerster had used in 1929 in *The American Scholar*. Finally, he maintained that the primary purpose of "this departure in graduate study" was not to produce "masterpieces of imaginative and critical literature," but "to give all types of literary students a rigorous and appropriate discipline," so that the majority of students, who would become teachers rather than authors, could function more effectively in that profession.[6]

About this time, President Jessup called Foerster to his office and urged him to organize a national Conference on Creative Writing for the purpose

Norman Foerster, director of the School of Letters from 1930 to 1944, persuaded the University administration and the Board of Education to accept the creative dissertation for the doctor of philosophy degree.

of making known the program to the general public. Taking place on October 29, 30, and 31 of 1931, the conference was the first of several during the 1930s to draw national attention to Iowa's innovational writing program. Speakers included: Dean Addison Hibbard of Northwestern University; Edwin Ford Piper of the University of Iowa; Zona Gale, Pulitzer Prize-winning short story writer and novelist from Wisconsin; Ruth Suckow, Iowa author from Hawarden; journalist Gerald W. Johnson of the University of North Carolina; Gorham B. Munson, New York critic, literary agent, and one-time new humanist; Irving B. Richman, Iowa historian; and Floyd Dell, who voiced a dissenting point of view by vigorously asserting that "all writing was the expression of an inner urge which could not be channelled by education and which lost its validity the moment it was subjected to such programs as were proposed by universities."[7]

Foerster himself spoke on the current rift between the American author and the university and announced his hopes for "a course which should give the creative writer the tools of literature without stifling his initiative."[8] He also commented on the requirements of the imaginative dissertation, which should "be published under reputable auspices." While Foerster would have liked this stipulation to have been a formal requirement, it was not. His intention, as one can infer from the following list of requirements, was both to establish high standards and to link creative endeavor with academic respectability:

> . . . first, that it illustrates the writer's proficiency in technique, his ability to discover and control a mode of expression suited to what he has to say; and, secondly, that it illustrates the writer's possession of creative energy, the sort of energy that distinguishes the really promising young author, who writes with a certain authority and seems to promise continuous growth. So much we have a right to ask of candidates of our highest degree.

Foerster was also careful to acknowledge the limits of the university's jurisdiction:

> But we have no right to go on to prescribe the direction to be taken by the writer's energy, the view of life for which he is seeking to find a fit vehicle, the particular ism to which he consciously or unconsciously adheres. He must be free to find himself, or to hang himself. At most we can demand only a certain unity of vision, a certain inner clearness as to his purpose.[9]

After the Conference on Creative Writing, Foerster spoke with Jessup about bringing recognized writers to campus "more or less to live with a selected group of promising writers." Foerster later recalled:

I proposed Robert Frost as the first visitor, remembering his long service in various institutions, especially Amherst, but Jessup promptly tossed this idea aside on the ground that Frost was "old hat." My next nominee was Steven *(sic)* Vincent Benét, at that time very widely popular. Far from being "old hat," I found when I met him at the railroad station he was appalled at the prospect of doing something he had never done before, and maybe I was equally embarrassed because I had never been in charge of such a situation before. However, after he reached my home, and we had had a talk after dinner we jointly explored the possibilities and by the time he left town, roughly about two weeks later, he had made a great success of his mission.[10]

Over the next few years, the University—following the lead of Iowa City's writers' clubs—sponsored readings by a number of recognized writers. Stephen Vincent Benét returned to campus in 1935 and 1938, Archibald MacLeish spoke to Edwin Ford Piper's classes in 1938, and eleven writers "of national repute" participated in the special "writers' workshops" of 1939.

During this period, there were indications that regionalism was becoming more exclusive and restrictive in its animating ideology. Midwestern literary regionalism, under the banner of John T. Frederick's the *Midland*, had gone beyond Josiah Royce's notion of place, which emanated from a fundamental faith in the intrinsic value of locale, and beyond his basic belief in the inherent diversity of American life. The movement had acquired a more aggressive and partisan flavor when it adopted its distinctly anti-urbanist stance. Like the broader ideological polarization that characterized American political and economic thought during the "pink decade," the voices raised in support of the regionalist cause after 1930 seemed to speak in notably harsher tones. In a 1931 article entitled "Misrepresentative Fiction," for example, Sam Sloan defended the values of rural living, the qualities of small-town life, and the cultural sophistication of the Midwest, and attacked the region's one-time residents who had become expatriate critics "like the birds that foul their own nests."[11] A few years later, the *Saturday Review of Literature* printed a pair of articles by Joseph E. Baker and Paul Robert Beath that advanced the pro and con arguments of regionalism in the context of a cultural conflict pitting America against New York. Interestingly enough, each writer accused the opposite side of narrow provincialism, preoccupation with mediocrity, and denial of the "Great Tradition" (in Matthew Arnold's sense of the phrase).[12]

Perhaps the best means of getting to the heart of the heightening controversy is to consider the thesis of Grant Wood's essay, "Revolt Against the City" (1935), allegedly ghost-written by Frank Luther Mott.[13] In this essay, the case "against the domination exercised over art and letters and over much of our thinking and living by Eastern capitals of finance and politics" is presented in an historical context:

> The dominant factor in American social history during the latter part of that [the nineteenth] century is generally recognized as being the growth of large cities. . . . This urban growth, whose tremendous power was so effective upon the whole of American society, served, as far as art was concerned, to tighten the grip of traditional imitativeness, for the cities were far less typically American than the frontier areas whose power they usurped. Not only were they the seats of the colonial spirit, but they were inimical to whatever was new, original and alive in the truly American spirit.[14]

In Grant Wood's view, the "definite swing" to regionalism had been given new impetus by the economic austerity of the 1930s, which reasserted and justified the agrarian ideal of self-reliance:

> . . . sweeping changes have come over American culture in the last few years. The Great Depression has taught us many things, and not the least of them is self-reliance. It has thrown down the Tower of Babel erected in the years of a false prosperity; it has sent men and women back to the land; it has caused us to rediscover some of the old frontier values, it has thrown us back upon certain true and fundamental things which are distinctively ours to use and to exploit.[15]

The impact of the regionalist movement was not confined to developments in literature. Under the direction of Hallie Flanagan, a network of regional theaters was organized in 1935 as a WPA project designed to put some 10,000 people back to work. E. C. Mabie was appointed regional director for the Midwest with the idea that Iowa City would become the regional center.[16] In the same year, Grant Wood was speaking out in favor of a similar program in art instruction, even going so far as to declare: "I believe the hope of a native American art lies in the development of regional art centers and the competition between them. It seems the only way to the building up of an honestly art-conscious America."[17]

Although new humanist ideology had little in common with the concerns of the regionalists, Foerster's emphasis on the legitimacy of creative writing within the academic community was welcomed by men like Edwin Ford Piper and Frank Luther Mott. In this regard he became something of an ally. Nevertheless, ideological differences remained. They were perhaps nowhere more evident than in Grant Wood's response to a definition of regionalism which was formulated by Foerster and a group of his

---

students and then submitted to Wood for comment. The definition by Foerster and his students read:

> Revolting against domination by the city (especially New York), against industrial civilization, against cultural nationalism and cosmopolitanism, and against an abstract humanism—all of them conceived as making for an artificial rootless literature—regionalism seeks to direct preponderating attention to the natural landscape, human geography, and cultural life and mark off particular areas of the country from other areas, in the belief that writers who draw from their own experience and the life they know best are more likely to attain universal values than those who do not.

To which Grant Wood suggested the following amendments:

> In this country, Regionalism has taken the form of a revolt against the cultural domination of the city (particularly New York) and the tendency of metropolitan cliques to lay more emphasis on artificial precepts than on more vital human experience. It is not, to my knowledge, a revolt against industrial civilization (in the William Morris sense), though it has re-emphasized the fact that America is agrarian as well as industrial. It has been a revolt against cultural nationalism—that is the tendency of artists to ignore or deny the fact that there are important differences, psychologically and otherwise, between the various regions of America. But this does not mean that Regionalism, in turn, advocates a concentration on local peculiarities; such an approach results in anecdotalism and local color.

Wood then volunteered a pointed distinction between the regionalist perspective and the general approach of Foerster and the new humanists:

> Regionalism, I believe, would denote a revolt against the tendencies of the Literary Humanism which you represent, to lay (what seems to me) disproportionate emphasis on cultures of the remote past and to remain aristocratically aloof from the life of the people at large. [18]

In the mind of at least one prominent regionalist, then, the thrust of Foerster's new humanism ran counter to the essence of the regionalist spirit.

Foerster's presence on the Iowa campus created for the regionalists a problem of divided loyalties. Because of a common commitment to the educational value of creative writing, the regionalists generally supported Foerster's endeavors. But when President Jessup suggested the nationwide Conference on Creative Writing to signal the initiation of Foerster's new program, Frank Luther Mott was opposed to the idea of making that single event serve also as the regional conference he had for some time been planning. Instead, he suggested separate conferences, the second to be a distinctively Iowa gathering of writers. Following the meeting at which Jessup made his proposal, Mott wrote to him:

> I think that it would be better to have two conferences than to try to accommodate the variety of aims which were expressed in your office to one meeting. . . . If . . . we combine the conference of Iowa authors with this other conference I feel sure that the more local and provincial side of the matter will get little attention. I think that Iowa would not be neglected in the larger conference but certainly it would not have the spotlight.

For the distinctively Iowa conference, Mott envisioned a gathering of writers reminiscent of the 1914 Iowa Authors' Homecoming:

> My idea would be to bring back as many Iowa writers to the state as possible and have a kind of Iowa literary field day in which the state's literary achievement should be celebrated and the possibilities for literary use of Iowa materials and the probabilities of future developments should be discussed. I cannot be sure just what writers we could induce to come to this conference but I do think it would be worth trying. I feel that we have a certain responsibility and loyalty to the state in its literary phases.[19]

As Mott wished, two conferences were in fact organized. Both Piper and Mott were active participants in Foerster's event, but they were unwilling to abandon the idea of a separate celebration of Iowa's literary achievement. Although it was four years in coming, the Iowa Literary Caucus was held April 26 and 27, 1935.[20]

As for the curriculum of the Program in Creative Writing during Foerster's tenure, no substantive changes were made. Frank Luther Mott continued to teach his short story course, Leigh Sowers his course in "Playwriting," Edwin Ford Piper his course in "Advanced Composition" (which involved practice in verse writing), and John T. Frederick would no doubt have continued to teach his course in "Advanced Short Story" had he not left for Chicago. The only change was in appearance. To each of the continuing courses was added the prefix, "Imaginative Writing." Likewise, the title of the required course in composition, "Constructive Rhetoric," was changed to "Art of Writing."[21]

The growing reputation of the University of Iowa's Department of English was another factor in the program's development. Foerster, who was responsible for shifting the department's emphasis from a traditional interest in historical scholarship and literary history to a concentration on literary criticism, enhanced the department's stature by adding Austin Warren and René Wellek to the faculty in 1939. In the field of literary theory, the department soon became one of the most highly esteemed in the country. Moreover, Foerster's widely used college anthology, *American Poetry and Prose* (1934), also contributed to the department's reputation, as did the well respected literary magazine, *American Prefaces*, which was published on the Iowa campus from 1935 until 1943.

During the 1930s, young talented writers were attracted to Iowa City not only as a result of the department's prominent faculty, but also because of early successes in publishing on the part of the program's students and graduates. The number of publications by the first students who submitted creative theses and dissertations under the new program was impressive and it helped to draw nation-wide attention to the program.[22] Of the first recipients of the creative M.A., Wallace Stegner published *Remembering Laughter* (1937), which won the Little Brown Novelette Prize, as well as five additional book-length publications in the next six years. Paul Engle, who had won the Yale Series of Younger Poets Award for *Worn Earth* in 1932, soon published three more books of poems and a novel. Another participant in the program, Margaret Walker Alexander, a black woman, also won the Yale Series Award for *For My People* (1940), a volume of verse submitted as her master's thesis.[23] Of the early recipients of the creative Ph.D., Henry Wilson, Ross Taylor, and Helene Magaret succeeded in finding publishers for the work they had submitted as dissertations.

In a four-year period (from 1937 to 1941), seven books written by students in the Workshop were issued by leading American publishers, and this is to say nothing of the numerous poems, stories, and essays that were appearing regularly in magazines.[24] Similarly, Robert Whitehand, who in 1941 was the first student to receive an M.F.A. (Master of Fine Arts) degree in creative writing, had earlier been honored by Edward J. O'Brien, who had dedicated his 1936 volume of *Best Short Stories* to Whitehand, calling him America's "most promising young writer."[25] Whitehand submitted a play for his thesis, entitled *Prelude to '76* (which was awarded $500 in a national play contest), and a group of short stories entitled *The First Thirteen* (all of which appeared in magazines, several in book form, with some published in Europe.)[26]

According to the Workshop's first director, Wilbur Schramm, the term "Writers' Workshop" was first used in reference to Edwin Ford Piper's graduate writing seminar, which was officially called "Imaginative Writing: Advanced." The name also was applied to a popular summer extension of Piper's regular graduate seminar, a course referred to both as the "writers' workshop" and the "summer workshop." Before long the entire program came to be called the "Writers' Workshop." As Schramm later recalled:

"People came to work with the Writers Workshop. They submitted their trial manuscripts by mail to the Writers Workshop. . . . The name, in other words, went much farther than we ever expected or intended."[27]

When the "summer workshop" course was expanded to a full-scale symposium in 1939, the name was used officially for the first time. The following headline appeared in the March 9 issue of the *Daily Iowan*: "Noted Authors To Meet Here; Writers' Workshop To Be Feature of '39 Summer Term," and the article explained: "A writers' workshop where students can do work toward publication aided by visiting authors of national reputation has been scheduled by the university for the 1939 summer session." In a second article that appeared two days later, it was announced that "eleven writers of national repute" would be visiting the campus during the term, some staying only briefly, others returning for more than one appearance, some appearing only to lecture or conduct round tables, and many acting as members of the summer staff. The featured writers were: Louis Adamic, Donald Davidson, Josephine Johnson, Paul Engle, Eric Knight, Herbert Krause, John T. Frederick, John G. Neihardt, Wallace Stegner, Ruth Suckow, and Winifred Van Etten.[28] The article described the series of events compromising the "writers' workshops" as "the fourth innovation announced for the 1939 'greater' summer session." The other three were a festival of fine arts, a management course for industrialists, and a course in six-man football.

The courses in creative writing to be offered that fall were likewise grouped for the first time under the new heading, "Writers' Workshop," in the 1939–40 University *Catalogue*. The category was described briefly:

> Group conferences and individual conferences. Consult Professor Schramm for permission to register. Associate Professor Schramm, Professor Mott; Associate Professor Sowers; Mr. Engle; Mr. Knight.[29]

In the same year that the term, "Writers' Workshop," was first used officially, the "Imaginative Writing" prefixes were dropped from the course titles and the introductory courses were called "Writing Fiction" and "Writing Poetry." The former course was taught in the first semester by Jack Boone and in the second by Eric Knight, and the latter was taught by Paul Engle. In the 1940–41 University *Catalogue* the same grouping, descriptions, and hierarchy were listed, with one exception—Robert Penn Warren, who was a visiting lecturer during the second semester, replaced Eric Knight on the regular Workshop staff.

Although the general grouping of creative writing courses was comparable to the Workshop's organization today, the administration of these courses was more flexible. The following is a description of how the Workshop was then organized:

Each year 25 or 30 students are admitted to the Workshop. Instruction is tailor-made to the individual. At first, the student holds weekly conferences with Prof. Wilbur Schramm, director of the Workshop. These conferences may last thirty minutes or several hours, according to the problems presented. Poets soon consult Paul Engle, playwrights Prof. Leigh Sowers, some of the prose writers Prof. Frank L. Mott. As the students develop they are organized into small groups which meet weekly or bi-weekly. The more expert a student becomes, the less need he has of frequent conferences and meetings, and the more time he needs for his own writing. The most envied group in the Workshop is the "top ten" who meet fortnightly at the homes of Schramm and Engle.[30]

In addition to the regular Workshop organization, there were two extensions or outgrowths of the regular Workshop: the Saturday Class Workshop, which was designed for a limited group from Iowa and surrounding states, and the Workshop of the Air, which consisted of lectures over WSUI radio for the benefit of writers and people who were interested in writing but unable to come to Iowa City.[31]

The Summer Workshop of 1941 was the expanding program's last special event before the bombing of Pearl Harbor and entry of the United States into World War II. In addition to the Workshop seminar and courses in fiction and magazine writing, the following activities were advertised:

There will be lectures on the making of poetry by Mr. Frost and Mr. Engle, on the making of fiction by Mr. Warren, Miss Suckow, and Mr. Stegner, on the craft of the critic by Mr. Foerster, on the problems of editing by Mr. Schramm, on the moving picture (illustrated by films of historical importance) by Mr. Knight. Station WSUI offers an opportunity for practical experience in radio; the magazine *American Prefaces* for experience in editorial work; the University Theatre for experience in play production. Such distinguished men as Hardin Craig, Fletcher Martin, Grant Wood, and Thompson Stone will teach courses in literature and the other arts, and the summer session will be unusually rich in public lectures, concerts, and exhibitions of art.[32]

During the war, the program, like the University as a whole, suffered a cutback in students and a reduction in activities.[33]

In light of this interplay between the voices of change and the impetus of tradition, it can be seen that the Writers' Workshop came into being not as the result of any single force or the contribution of any one individual. Indeed, the tenuous alliance between Foerster and the regionalists seems no more or less significant than the literary atmosphere nurtured by Iowa City's long succession of writers' clubs or the impact of the lecture by

Josiah Royce or the inspiration engendered by the *Midland*. Nevertheless, it seems reasonable to conclude that, while the full status accorded the imagination by Norman Foerster opened the doors of the academy, the emergence of the Writers' Workshop remained essentially an Iowa phenomenon, deriving its impetus from the last throes of the regionalist movement.

Beyond the course offerings, principal figures, factors, and events in the emergence of the Writers' Workshop, the element of attitude should be recognized. Whether nurtured by some ineffable spirit of place or derived from the feeling of self-worth that comes from small-town existence, an undeniable ambience grew up among the community of people who were devoted to artistic endeavor. Robert Penn Warren tried to put his finger on this attitude when he recalled years later:

> The one thing that struck me most about my first visit was the pervasive and communal literary sense—if one may call it that, the interpenetration of interests among faculty (or a number of the faculty) and students, not only "writing students" but many of the brightest graduate students. . . . What I am getting at here is how people of such basically different interests and trainings could find a common ground, fruitful for all. I am sure that most of those people never had found anything like that before, nor have found anything like it since. And something of this carried over into the class. It was a humane occasion, touching on all sorts of concerns without ever forgetting the main one.[34]

As Wilbur Schramm later recalled, this unique spirit of cooperation played a key role in the emergence of the Writers' Workshop:

> In fact, if there was any characteristic of the Workshop I remember, it was the number of people who became interested and helped—quietly or loudly. . . . It seemed like an idea whose time had come. People gathered around and *wanted* to help. . . . So anything that happened in the Workshop could hardly be ascribed to one person, and usually involved several.[35]

Because of many factors, not the least of which was the irrepressible enthusiasm that emanates from creative endeavor, the gap between the regionalists and Foerster was bridged and the "idea whose time had come" was realized.

NOTES

1   George F. Kay, letter to Walter A. Jessup, April 15, 1930, Foerster Papers, University of Iowa Archives, Iowa City.

2   Norman Foerster, letter to John C. Gerber, February 16, 1968, Foerster Papers, University of Iowa Archives, Iowa City.

3   Frank Luther Mott, letter to Walter A. Jessup, November 7, 1930, Presidents' Correspondence, 1930–31, folder no. 62, University of Iowa Archives, Iowa City.

4   Foerster, letter to Gerber.

5   "Iowa's School of Letters Admits Imaginative, Critical Writing for Ph.D. Thesis," *Daily Iowan* (March 26, 1931), p. 3.

6   *Ibid.*

7   Harry Hansen, "The Iowa Writers' Conference," *Saturday Review of Literature* (November 21, 1931), 315.

8   *Ibid.*

9   *Ibid.*

10   Foerster, letter to Gerber.

11   Sam Sloan, "Misrepresentative Fiction," *Palimpsest,* 12 (February 1931), 47–48. In that article, Sam Sloan wrote:

> Nobody who keeps abreast of the public prints can fail to realize the snobbish, the contemptuous, the God-Almighty attitude toward the Middle West that exists among some, not most, Easterners to-day. There have been striking proofs of it in the last two or three years and they are doubtless fresh in the minds of all of you. Heywood Broun has described us as "the land of the Babbitts." Senator Grundy has been telling us we belong to the "backward states." Senator Moses has been a little franker by dubbing us "sons of wild jackasses."
>
> That this attitude should exist in the New England States does not strike me as strange; it is, in reality a normal, a natural outgrowth of the novels written by one-time or expatriate Middle Westerners who are like the birds that foul their own nests.

12   Joseph E. Baker and Paul Robert Beath, "Regionalism: Pro and Con; Four Arguments for Regionalism and Four Fallacies of Regionalism," *Saturday Review of Literature* (November 28, 1936), 3, 4, 14, 16.
There were other indications that regionalism was becoming more firmly established. In 1935, Frank Luther Mott founded the Whirling World Series, a series of brochures or pamphlets featuring the works of regional authors. Grant Wood's essay, "Revolt Against the City," Paul Green's new play, "Shroud My Body Down," Edwin Ford Piper's cycle of sonnets on Chaucer and Chaucerian characters, and Hamlin Garland's Iowa poems were published as the first four numbers. In 1936 and for a few years thereafter, Wilbur Schramm taught a course entitled "Literature of the Middle West" and in 1939 Luella Wright taught "Cultural

Developments in Iowa," which explored cultural influences and backgrounds of various Iowa communities.

13   The essay was published in pamphlet form in 1935 by the Clio Press as part of the Whirling World Series. In his dissertation, entitled "Frank Luther Mott: Journalism Educator," University of Missouri, Columbia, 1968, Max Lawrence Marshall quotes Mott's daughter, Mildred Mott Wedel: "Grant Wood did not write with ease, so Pops did the actual writing, according to my understanding, after careful discussion of just what Wood wanted said . . . and fundamentally, it was Wood's creation" (p. 241).

14   Grant Wood, *Revolt Against the City*. Whirling World Series 1 (Iowa City: Clio Press, 1935), p. 43.

15   *Ibid.*, pp. 18–19.

16   See Hallie Flanagan Davis, *Arena* (New York: Duell, Sloan and Pearce, 1940).

17   Wood, *Revolt*, p. 43.

18   Grant Wood, "A Definition of Regionalism," *Books at Iowa*, 3 (November 1965), 3–4.

19   Mott, letter to Walter Jessup.

20   In 1932, Mott had accepted an office in the Iowa Authors Club and he now saw an opportunity to integrate an activity of the club with the Iowa conference. He accordingly wrote the new University President Eugene Gilmore in November 1934:

> I am very anxious to establish closer correlation between the Iowa Authors Club, which includes most of the active writing men and women of Iowa, with the University and its activities. This organization has, ever since I have known it, centered in Des Moines and its meetings have always been held there. Since a reorganization two years ago, the control of the club has passed largely out of the hands of Des Moines people and there is not only a willingness but an anxiety to hold one of its chief meetings of the year at Iowa City.
>
> What we should like to do is to hold a two-day meeting of the club at Iowa City about May 1 or 2, 1935. In order to make this a success it will be necessary to have a nationally important author who can make a good speech and who will not only take part in the general program of the club's meeting but give a University lecture in the auditorium of Macbride Hall. The man we have fixed upon is Stephen Vincent Benet, the poet and novelist, and author of the Pulitzer prize poem *John Brown's Body*, and other important works. [Mott, letter to Eugene Gilmore, November 22, 1934, Presidents' Correspondence, folder no. 62.]

In addition to Stephen Vincent Benét's lecture on April 26, activities of the Iowa Literary Caucus included a series of "Round Table" discussions held in the stately Senate Chamber of Old Capitol. Edwin Ford Piper presided over the Poetry Round Table, whose panel (comprised of Jay Sigmund, Lewis Worthington Smith, James Hearst, Raymond Kresensky, Don Farran, and others) addressed the questions: "The Art and the 'Isms'; The Poet and His Subject; The Ungentle Reader; The Critics." The magazine Writing Round Table, presided over by Elmer T. Peterson (editor of *Better Homes and Gardens*) with Johnson Brigham, Dorothy Pownall, John

E. Briggs, and Elizabeth M. Bray as participants, considered the following questions: "What is the best way to develop a market for fact articles? What is the
market for poetry? What is the advantage of having a broker? Should an article be
accompanied by a long covering letter?" Frank Luther Mott presided over a series
of brief talks by representatives of Iowa's "little magazines," which included
Dubuque Dial, Tanager, Palimpsest, Hinterland, Husk, Sketch, and *American Prefaces.*
Finally, John Towner Frederick returned to campus to lead Elmer T. Peterson,
Thomas Duncan, Josephine Donovan, and Johnson Brigham in discussing these
topics: "Should the novelist tell a story? The status of regionalism; Can fiction
writing be taught?" for the Fiction Round Table. (Information based on printed
program, "Iowa Literary Caucus, April 26 and 27, 1935, Iowa City, Iowa," copy in
Workshop Files, University of Iowa Archives, Iowa City.)

21   1930–31 *University of Iowa Catalogue,* pp. 230–31.

22   The first creative master's thesis—a collection of poems, entitled *Paisley Shawl,*
submitted by Mary Roberts in 1931—was followed in February of 1932 by Wallace
Stegner's *Bloodstain and Other Stories;* in June of 1932 by Paul Engle's *One Slim
Feather,* a book of poems; Donald Freerer's *Slag,* an original three-act play; Erling
Larsen's *The Earth Abideth,* a novel; and Donald MacRae's *The Dancing Lesson,* a
group of short stories. The first creative doctoral dissertation, entitled *Of Lunar
Kingdoms* (a group of informal essays), was submitted by Henry Wilson in 1935;
followed in 1936 by Winn Zeller's *A Soul Went Out in Fire,* a tragedy; in 1937 by
David Ash's *Liberty Hall,* a novel; in 1938 by Ross Taylor's *Brazos,* a novel; and in
1940 by Jack Bryan's *Young in the City;* Helene Magaret's *Father De Smet,* a biography; and Janet Piper's *The Bitter Root,* which was the first book of poems to be
submitted as a doctoral dissertation.

23   In 1962, Margaret Walker Alexander returned to the University of Iowa, in
spite of the unhappiness she had experienced as a student in the late thirties. She
returned to work on a Ph.D. and in 1965 she submitted as her doctoral dissertation
the manuscript, *Jubilee,* an historical novel set in the Civil War. In a letter to Paul
Engle, dated march 21, 1973, she recalled her experience at Iowa in this way:

> Of course you know I never meant to go back. I suffered a lot of trauma that
> year through no one's fault other than my own, but I was miserable and I kept
> thinking how awful it was not to have *any* money and being ill all the time,
> despondent and depressed to the point of tears. That commencement night
> August 1940 I packed my trunk and managed to get it to the train station before
> midnight. When I left the next morning at five o'clock I vowed never to look
> back and never to go back there any more.
>
> That is why those three years I spent in Iowa City during the 1960's seem so
> miraculous. Of course, I had followed your advice to the letter, "Go out and
> live awhile and get yourself a job before you think about another degree."
> Once again I knocked on your door throwing my hat in first to see if you would
> let me enter that workshop again. After all those years of absolute silence you
> looked at a middle-aged woman and said yes again in more than words. You
> helped make it possible for me to come back, getting [me] a job, ways and
> means *again* because that is precisely what you did in 1939 and whether I
> seemed grateful or not, without a word of thanks you did it again! And you
> warned me that I would have to translate 100 lines of Virgil for that Ph.D. Latin
> requirement which I did, only God knows how! That is why 1962–63–64–65

were more like a dream than 1939–1940. Very rarely do people have a second chance to make good.

A copy of this letter is included in "Workshop Correspondence with Wilbers," no. 238, University of Iowa Archives, Iowa City.

24 Information based on *Theses and Dissertations, presented in the graduate college of the State University of Iowa, 1900–1950* (1952), compiled by Sarah Scott Edwards and edited by Pauline Cook, and on *University of Iowa News Bulletin* vol. 16 (January 1941). The seven published books were: Helene Magaret's *The Great Horse* (1937), a long narrative poem about the Mormon migration; Ross M. Taylor's *Brazos* (1938), a novel about Texas cattlemen; George Abbe's *Voices in the Square* (1938), a novel about a small New England town; Louise McNeill's *Gauley Mountain* (1930), a book of poems; Herbert Krause's *Wind Without Rain* (1939), a novel which won a $1,000 prize as best book of the year by a western author; Mildred Haun's *The Hawk's Done Gone* (1940), a novel of Tennessee mountain life; and Helen Magaret's *Father De Smet* (1940), a biography of a great missionary priest.

25 The M.F.A. program, designed to provide technical and professional experience for the artist in the fields of music, dramatic art, and art, was first listed in the 1937–38 University *Catalogue* and, in the 1938–39 *Catalogue*, the program was expanded to include creative writing. Today, the degree is awarded with far greater frequency than the Ph.D. with a creative dissertation.

26 Another student soon to become well known was Tennessee Williams, who was a junior transfer in the fall of 1937 and who was awarded a B.A. in the summer of 1938. However, the University of Iowa can claim little credit for his later success because he did poorly in his classes and did not participate in the graduate writing program.

27 Wilbur Schramm, letter to Paul Engle, August 10, 1976, copy included in "Workshop Correspondence with Wilbers," no. 225, University of Iowa Archives, Iowa City.

28 Louis Adamic, novelist, social critic, was author of such works as *Laughing in the Jungle, Native's Return, Dynamite,* and *My America;* Donald Davidson, leading southern regionalist and poet, professor of English at Vanderbilt University, was author of *Attack on Leviathan, Lee in the Mountains,* and *The Tall Men;* Josephine Johnson, one of America's leading women novelists, was winner of the Pulitzer Prize for her *Now in November;* Paul Engle, regular member of the Iowa staff, was the poet of such works as *Worn Earth, American Song,* and *Break the Heart's Anger;* Eric Knight, the English novelist, was author of the then recent, much-acclaimed novella, *The Flying Yorkshireman;* Herbert Krause was a graduate of the University of Iowa, whose novel *Wind Without Rain* had excited favorable comment that year; John T. Frederick, novelist, critic, and former editor of *Midland,* had been a teacher of writing at Iowa and Northwestern and was then professor at Notre Dame and book review editor of the Columbia Broadcasting system; John G. Neihardt was a poet and author of such epic poems as *The Song of Hugh Glass, Song of Three Friends,* and *Song of the Indian Wars;* Wallace Stegner, Iowa novelist, was winner of Little Brown's $2,500 prize for his *Remembering Laughter;* Ruth Suckow, Iowa novelist, was winner of the Pulitzer Prize for her Iowa novel, *The Folks;* and Winifred Van Etten was the novelist who won the $10,000 *Atlantic Monthly* prize with her novel, *I Am the Fox.*

It was also noted that Professor Edwin Ford Piper, "a member of the faculty of the university for more than 30 years," would offer "an introductory course in poetry, in addition to his regular thesis seminar," and that Professor Wilbur L. Schramm was "the chairman of the writer's project, a function of the school of letters"; and that Paul Engle was in charge of the poetry section, Professor Frank L. Mott was handling prose, and Professor Schramm fiction.

In September of 1940, on the occasion of Virgil Hancher's appointment as president of the University, *Time* reported that at Iowa they "believed that the way to learn about art was to produce it." To illustrate the point, the article offered the following laudatory description:

> Soon Iowa's husky pupils were enthusiastically painting, sculpting, writing, acting, composing. Scornful of second-hand scholarship, Iowa's teachers let students win their degrees by substituting for a traditional thesis an original novel, a painting, a performance in a play, a musical composition. Exclaimed critic Edward J. O'Brien *(Best Short Stories):* "Iowa City is the Athens of America." *Time* (September 23, 1940), 43.

29   1939–40 *University of Iowa Catalogue*, p. 213.

30   "Young Writers Are Producing in S.U.I. Workshop," *University of Iowa News Bulletin*, 16 (January 1941).

31   *Ibid.*

32   "The Summer Writers' Workshop," University of Iowa Publications, April 16, 1941, copy in "Writers' Workshop—Study and Teaching," University of Iowa Archives, Iowa City.

33   In January of 1943, Eric Knight, the Yorkshireman whose quick wit and penetrating insight were warmly appreciated by many of his students at Iowa, was killed in a plane crash when on a mission for U.S. Army Intelligence.

34   Robert Penn Warren, letter to Engle, September 1, 1976, copy included in "Workshop Correspondence with Wilbers," no. 228, University of Iowa Archives, Iowa City.

35   Schramm, letter to Engle, August 10, 1976, no. 225.

Profile of Wilbur Schramm
as First Director

WILBUR SCHRAMM's term as director of the Writers' Workshop was a brief but important one. He served from the time of Piper's death in May 1939, when he was asked to take over Piper's advanced seminar, until the end of the first semester of the school year 1941–42, when he requested a leave of absence to go to Washington as part of the war effort.

In the years since his involvement, Wilbur Schramm has downplayed the importance of his role as first director. He has asserted that at the time he suspected that his greatest talents were neither in writing fiction nor in teaching it, but in theory of communication, a field in which he subsequently distinguished himself. About the circumstances of his becoming the Workshop's director, he has written: "When he [Piper] died, suddenly of a heart attack, I had to take over. They should probably have gotten someone else at that time, and I rather expected them to; but I had a little while when no one else was there, and so had a lot of fun doing what I thought needed doing."[1] Despite such disclaimers, Wilbur Schramm's contribution to the development of the Writers' Workshop was significant. He played an important role as spokesman for the rationale of the program that was developing under Norman Foerster's aegis and was generally perceived by his students to be a dedicated and effective teacher.[2]

In articulating his argument for the creative writing program, Schramm provided a forceful extension and application of Foerster's thoughts on both the rightful status of the imagination within the academy and the importance of approaching literature from a humane rather than scientific point of view. *Literary Scholarship, Its Aims and Methods,* was published in 1941 as a collaborative effort by Norman Foerster, John C. McGalliard, René Wellek, Austin Warren, and Wilbur L. Schramm, with respective essays on "The Study of Letters," "Language," "Literary History," "Literary Criticism," and "Imaginative Writing." In his essay, Schramm addressed the unwholesome rift that had developed between the scholar and the writer by quoting Max Eastman, who described the "official viewpoint" as coming down to the opinion that "a poet in history is divine, but a poet in the next room is a joke." Also quoted was Allen Tate who once observed, "We study literature today from various historical points of view, as if nobody ever intended to write any more of it."[3] Schramm elaborated:

> Harvard meant a good deal to American literature one hundred years ago; now it means about as much as the New York subway. And I have heard it said regretfully in England that Oxford and Cambridge, with their long tradition of University poets—Spenser, Donne, Herrick, Herbert, Milton, Dryden, Gray, Wordsworth, Coleridge, Byron, Tennyson, Hopkins—have likewise fallen greatly in their importance to current literature. The universities were better for having had in their midst the men just mentioned.[4]

Corresponding to the argument that the university would benefit by the presence of practicing writers—who by their example might help raise the general competence of writing and who also would tend to make better teachers of literature because of their love of reading and their "inside" view of the art—was the argument that many writers could benefit from the experience provided by a university. For one thing, there was the basic issue of education: "The truth is, we have come to think of the author as an 'expresser,' and have lost sight of the fact that 'man thinking'—in the productions of great literature—precedes 'man expressing.' "[5] Another issue to be considered was the fact that by teaching, the writer was often relieved of the need for an outside means of support.

As for the practical question of how writing is taught, Schramm made the obvious point that "no university could undertake to turn out writers as it produces physicians, lawyers, chemists, and teachers." He observed that a man cannot be taught "to write, or for that matter, to practice any profession," but that "the teacher directs, aids, encourages; the student learns by his own effort."[6] The necessary program for the artist in the university, then, was simply to "open the riches of the university to the young writer":

> Let us be sure that the university takes seriously both the great books of the past and the important books of the present, that the student has leisure and opportunity to read them, think about them, talk about them with older men who have given years to understanding. Let us represent the other arts in the university by examples of their historical development and their present practice. Let us have natural scientists and social students ready to turn their particular kinds of light on the present. Let us have critics and historical scholars working beside the writer, practicing their particular approaches to his art.[7]

Wilbur Schramm became the first director of the Writers' Workshop in 1939. He supported the practicing writer in the university and defended the legitimacy of the creative doctoral dissertation.

Perhaps most important was that Schramm sought to convince his audience of the legitimacy of the creative doctoral dissertation at a time when many educators considered the practice irresponsible. He justified the idea on the basis of the rigor and intellectual effort involved:

> The discipline we have been describing is comparable both in quality and in severity with the discipline of any other advanced literary study. The graduate student would not find a good play, or novel, or book of verse an easy substitute for the usual thesis or dissertation.

Such a piece of imaginative writing would have to be based upon close, accurate observation and information; it would have to be composed with a feeling for words as expert as that of the linguist; it would require a series of judgments not unlike those of the literary critic, and by virtue of selection and organization would require quite as much "logic" as a difficult study in literary history.[8]

In addition to his role as spokesman, Schramm appears to have been quite effective as a teacher. He was exceptionally conscientious and personally committed to his students' development as writers. Some thirty-five years after working with him, one of his former students, John Hospers, wrote:

Wilbur Schramm . . . had a missionary zeal about writing, and he did everything in his power to bring out the best in his students, to elicit just the right image, to help them achieve maximum vividness and precision, to inject into the writing a feeling-tone and an atmosphere that was exactly right for the story. I seem to remember that he himself preferred a rather Hemingwayesque style, with overtones of Mark Twain, but he did not try to push his young writers into styles that were not natural to them; if they preferred to be expansive, he would let them be as Wolfesian as they wished, as long as they did not lose precision, a strong sense of atmosphere, sound character-development, and natural unstilted dialogue.[9]

In support of his contention that Schramm's "appetite for work was insatiable," Hospers related the following anecdote:

I remember, for example, a day when he received in the mail an alarmingly thick batch of manuscripts from the Writers' Guild of one small city in Iowa (which shall here be nameless). He had no professional obligation to read their material, and even I could see at that time that most of the stories and poems they submitted were bloody awful. He must have known it too, with much greater poignancy than I did, but he read them all just the same, without fee, commented on them in great detail, and sent them back.[10]

Another student of the period, Barbara Spargo, described her experience in Schramm's Workshop class in this way:

The entire fiction program was conducted by Wilbur Schramm on a very informal and entirely individual basis. He was always available for personal conferences, at least once a week in his office in the basement of University Hall.

Meetings of the Workshop as a whole (8–10 students) were not held at regularly scheduled times, but took place perhaps once a month whenever several members had something "ready" to present. Such group meetings were often held in Schramm's home where his big dog, Shakespeare, snored by the fireplace. The very attractive, Mrs. Schramm, served coffee and cookies. We watched four-year old, Mary Schramm, showing off for guests and being loved, too. Mary wrote poetry once in a while, and her dad was obviously proud to read it aloud to his students. Sometimes, he would ask for our comments on his own short stories. Windwagon Smith was the hero of an adventure series by that name which he sold to the very popular *Saturday Evening Post*. In those days, I was confident that Windwagon would establish Wilbur Schramm as a great American writer. Even today, I am still sorry that he laid Windwagon aside to become a recognized authority on television and mass media problems.[11]

Spargo also commented on Schramm's general approach to teaching and class work:

Of course, in the group meetings of the Workshop, the students read and "tore apart" each other's writings. The best in each student was brought out by Schramm through a combination of his own very warm and human personality, talent, imagination, and of the would-be writers. I believe he felt a serious commitment to help each student develop according to each one's abilities. He stressed that each person's writing should reflect something unique in that individual and represent a certain integrity of purpose, style, and content.

The importance of reading other writers was always emphasized. Schramm personally knew Wallace Stegner, and I recall considerable discussion of his fiction. Others I remember being talked about are Robert Penn Warren, Eric Knight, and Archibald MacLeish. Literary criticism in the academic sense was left to Norman Foerster's required course in the subject.[12]

Wilbur Schramm's dynamic personality and youthful enthusiasm enabled him to establish a special rapport with his students despite his stutter. He was, in fact, so young in appearance that one of his students once missed an interview with him because it never dawned on her that the "youngster" in the office with a group of graduate students was the professor she had been told to see.[13]

Perhaps the most revealing testimony on Schramm as a teacher and a man comes from Karsten Ohnstad, a blind student whom Schramm encouraged to write and helped to find the financial means of staying in school. At the end of his autobiographical work, *The World at My Finger Tips*, which he submitted as his M.A. thesis in 1942 and which was subsequently published by the Bobbs-Merrill Company, Ohnstad portrayed the turning point in his career as a writer:

> The class in which I immediately found myself was made up of young men of my own age, most of them graduate students from colleges and universities all over the nation. Several of them were writing novels. Homer had been a hero scout for the Carnegie Commission, traveling to all corners of the United States in search of heroes who deserved a decoration. Don had worked on a newspaper and written stories that had been published in the famous O'Brien collection. Tony had played in Chicago dance bands, and wrote fiction with a skill that almost extinguished my hopes of competing successfully. We met informally in Doctor Schramm's office, smoked cigarettes, drank black coffee, and criticized the original stories which members of the group read. I sat quietly by the wall, overwhelmed. I dared not bring anything that I had written, to be read aloud.
>
> It was already November. As I wrote each day, I found that some of the anecdotes which I had heard at the School for the Blind and those in which I had taken a part were forming themselves into an article. I rearranged it several times, polished it, and brought it to class. I was afraid to have it read, but I had to get started on my thesis. The criticism would help. If I did not get my degree in the spring, the whole year would be wasted. The other men smoked and listened while Joe read my article aloud. I wondered, fearfully, what thoughts were running through their minds. Joe finished. Out of deference for my blindness, I thought, no one offered any scathing criticism. I waited for the ax to fall.
>
> "Ohnstad," Doctor Schramm said, turning to me with a smile in his voice. "You ought to write a book."[14]

As a final note on Schramm as teacher, it is possible to get a feeling for his approach to the technique of writing from *The Story Workshop* (1938), a textbook Schramm wrote for developing writers. The book is based on the "disarmingly simple" formula that in order to write a good short story a "writer must be able to make a penetrating observation about life, and he must be able to convey that observation, in an interesting narrative form, to a reader."[15] In this work, Schramm considers the questions of topic, delineation of character, dialogue, narrative, and the coherence of the final product. Each section includes examples of successful short stories by well known writers which are presented along with occasional marginal comments on the various effects and devices employed in the selections. Schramm's general approach in the textbook is to point out the basic components of a work of fiction and to stress the relative importance of each. As one might expect of such a conscientious reader of student work, Schramm emphasizes the need for close reading and attention to language.

In January 1942, Wilbur Schramm requested a leave of absence for war service in Washington. At that time, Paul Engle, who had joined the faculty as a lecturer in 1937, was appointed acting director. Upon his return to Iowa at the end of 1943, Schramm did not ask to be reinstated in his former position because his interests had shifted somewhat during the intervening time and because he found the Workshop in good hands upon his return:

> When I was ready to come back to Iowa, my experience with the new communication scholars—Hovland, Lazarsfeld, Lasswell, and so forth—had changed my research interests. I had run some large programs, and it was assumed—although, I must say, never proved—that I had some administrative abilities. Therefore, when the time of return came I was offered several administrative jobs in the University, including the position as Director of Libraries. Paul was doing a brilliant job as head of the writing program, and it would have seemed ridiculous to go back to what I had been doing. The Directorship of the small School of Journalism became vacant when my good friend, Frank Mott (who had always been a staunch supporter of the Workshop) went to Missouri as Dean. That position was offered to me, and I took it. [16]

Before leaving Iowa for good in the summer of 1947 for the University of Illinois, Schramm performed one last service for the Workshop. In 1945, acting in his capacity as head of the Journalism School, he helped to establish the University of Iowa's Typographic Laboratory. Schramm persuaded Carroll Coleman, a highly esteemed small press proprietor in Muscatine, to come to Iowa City with his letterpress operation (The Prairie Press) and to serve as director of the new laboratory. He arranged for funding of the project with T. Henry Foster (a wealthy book collector from Ottumwa). In this way, Schramm played a crucial role in founding a small press movement that has continued to flourish in Iowa City under the successive leadership of Harry Duncan of the Cummington Press, Kim Merker of the Stone Wall Press and Windhover Press, Kay Amert and Howard Zimmon of the Seamark Press, and many others. [17] Over the years, Iowa City's dense concentration of small press proprietors—who consider a book's appearance in itself a work of art and who generally concern themselves with literary rather than commercial ventures—has been one of the city's more important assets for the young writer in search of a publisher.

In assessing Wilbur Schramm's impact on the development of the Writers' Workshop, it is important to recognize that his appointment as director stands as a shift in the program's direction. Beyond the significance of his work to make the creative Ph.D. academically respectable and beyond his effectiveness as a teacher, there were important ramifications to Schramm's appointment. Until then, the program's faculty was weighted in favor of the regionalists. But with Edwin Ford Piper's death and Schramm's appointment as director of the Writers' Workshop, the scales were tipped in favor of a younger faculty whose primary allegiance was to Norman Foerster.

It is equally significant that Edwin Ford Piper, despite his senior status, had never been designated director of the program. Foerster's desire to prevent the Workshop from becoming too closely associated with the regionalists was no doubt a factor here. According to Wilbur Schramm, the regionalists no longer represented "the new and exciting things" that were going on in the 1930s. He has written:

> It was wonderful to have Grant Wood there, and Thomas Hart Benton coming frequently to visit him. It was pleasant to have Ruth Suckow close by. And all of us loved Edwin Ford Piper. But the people we brought in to talk with our students were Robert Penn Warren and Donald Davidson and Robert Frost and Archibald MacLeish and Gertrude Stein (she never quite made it because of a snowstorm, but we tried). The poets our young writers would be likely to read would not be Neihardt, but rather Eliot and Auden and Rilke and later lesser known people who were far from the regionalists of the 20's. . . . We obviously were friendly with the regionalists because they were the only group of creative writers and painters widely known in the region at the time. But all the currents were headed elsewhere. Foerster was leading a parade of students back to Plato and Aristotle and across the channel to Saint Beuve and French explication. The Department of Art was bringing in visiting artists even during Grant Wood's time who represented a vastly different concept of painting from Grant's. It seems reasonable to me, then, that Mr. Piper must have felt a bit out of the main stream. He had been a member of a very orthodox English department; he found those patterns being torn up and the department broadening out. He must have felt—as all we elders do—the impatience and ambition of vigorous young fellows like Paul [Engle] and Wally Stegner and me, whose eyes were mostly on new writers, new art, and new ways.

As for Piper's status, Schramm explained:

> I can say this, that as long as Mr. Piper was living and healthy, he was

and would have been regarded as the senior member of the writing staff. He could have done anything he wanted to. I doubt that he wanted to build up the kind of program that would bring in young talented writers from all over the country, or start a journal, or offer a doctorate that, under suitable conditions, might be earned with a creative dissertation. That was not his way, and his energies at the time would not have led him in those directions. But as long as he was there, he was senior, he was respected, I and others in the program deferred to him; and I, for one, tried to talk over with him any new plans for the writing program I had in mind.[18]

Although Wilbur Schramm was not in total accord with Foerster's new humanist thought and concerns, he shared his conviction that the Writers' Workshop should grow in the direction of a national rather than regional institution.

NOTES

1 Wilbur Schramm, letter to Paul Engle, August 10, 1976, copy included in "Workshop Correspondence with Wilbers," no. 225, University of Iowa Archives, Iowa City.

2 An early project of Schramm's seems to reveal an approach to creative writing that was at once imaginative and scientific. In April of 1934, Schramm was awarded a fellowship for the study of poetical versification of phonophotography and a year later he gave a demonstration of a rhythm graph, a means of charting the medley schemes of verse. See "Approaches to a Science of English Verse," *University of Iowa Studies, Series on Aims and Progress of Research* 46 (April 15, 1935), and Carl Seashore and Schramm, "Drive and Intensity in English Tetrameter Verse," *Philological Quarterly*, 13 (January 1934), 65–73.

3 Schramm, "Imaginative Writing," *Literary Scholarship, Its Aims and Methods*, by Norman Foerster, John C. McGalliard, René Wellek, Austin Warren, and Wilbur L. Schramm (Chapel Hill: University of North Carolina Press, 1941), pp. 178–79.

4 *Ibid.*, p. 211.

5 *Ibid.*, p. 207.

6 *Ibid.*, p. 198.

7 *Ibid.*, p. 209.

8 *Ibid.*, p. 190.

9 John Hospers, letter to Jean Wylder, April 1973, copy included in "Workshop Correspondence with Wilbers," no. 168, University of Iowa Archives, Iowa City.

10   *Ibid.*

11   Barbara Spargo, letter to the author, February 16, 1976, "Workshop Correspondence with Wilbers," no. 6, University of Iowa Archives, Iowa City.

12   *Ibid.*

13   The incident of the missed interview occurred to Ruth Bortin, who wrote of it in a letter to the author, April 21, 1976, no. 113. Barbara Spargo offered this description of Schramm in a letter to the author, February 16, 1976, no. 6:

> As for Schramm's appearance, I have heard many people on first meeting him remark, "His personality just *grabs* me!" His eyes were especially sincere, happy, and gentle. (Description such as this seems totally unsuccessful to me). In physical build, he was not a large man, hardly the football player type, but he had a certain "boyish" athletic bearing. His dark curly hair was generally rather tousled, and his clothes comfortably casual; he smoked a pipe.

14   Karsten Ohnstad, *The World at My Finger Tips* (Indianapolis, New York: Bobbs-Merrill, 1942), pp. 338-39.

15   Schramm, *The Story Workshop* (Boston: Little, Brown, 1938), p. v.

16   Schramm, letter to Engle.

17   Since Carroll Coleman's arrival, more than fifteen small presses have operated in Iowa City, giving the town a density of small presses second only perhaps to Boston and Los Angeles. Among others, they have included: Carroll Coleman's Prairie Press, Harry Duncan's Cummington Press, Kim Merker's Stone Wall Press and Windhover Press, Gerald Stevenson's Qara Press, Kay Amert and Howard Zimmon's Seamark Press, Bonnie O'Connell's Penumbra Press, Leigh McLellan's Meadow Press, Allan and Cinda Kornblum's Toothpaste Press, Lauren Geringer's Gehry Press, T. Hunter Wilson's Griffin Press, David Young's Pacific Inland Press, Stan Liedtke's Fire Mark Press, Al Buck and Brad Harvey's Ocotillo Press, Eric Olsen's Athanor Press, Lissa Lunning's Cyathus Press, and Chase Twitchell's Ausable Press—not to mention many other presses that have published only a few titles under their imprints.

18   Wilbur Schramm, letter to the author, April 15, 1977, "Workshop Correspondence with Wilbers," no. 254, University of Iowa Archives, Iowa City.

Profile of Norman Foerster

BEFORE COMING TO IOWA by way of the University of North Carolina, Norman Foerster was a student at Harvard, where he studied under Irving Babbitt and learned the creed of the new humanists. Like Babbitt and Paul Elmer More, Foerster was distressed by the growing influence of naturalism in early twentieth-century America and by the application of Darwinian and science-oriented approaches to the study of American letters. A traditionalist in his defense of a liberal education based on a broad study of the humanities, but a rebel in his conviction that both criticism and creative work should occupy a central position in higher education, Norman Foerster was himself a paradox.

As revealed in his brief work, *The American Scholar* (1929), his chief complaint against the state of American letters was that American scholars were giving undue emphasis to literary history rather than attending to literature itself. The way Foerster saw it, many scholars were doing nothing more than desperately keeping up with other scholars who immersed themselves in philology and minute historical research rather than studying the works themselves. It was a case of scholars contenting themselves with "living in other times and places" rather than "regarding time and place as obstacles to be overcome and surpassed, or disturbing factors to be eventually cancelled."[1] This "making history not a means but an end in itself" was producing a kind of "knowledge without thought," which Foerster defined as "the amassing of historical data unvitalized by reason and imagination in their deeper manifestations."[2] What was needed, Foerster felt, was a new commitment to the consideration of value and a restoration of "the traditional alliance of scholarship and criticism." It was the divorce between the scholar and the critic that was making American scholarship "narrowly mechanical and progressively tangential," and it was this same separation that was playing a major role in the disintegration of American education, for it was making the study of the humanities "scientific in an age already blinded with excess of scientific light, an age that is groping in vain for such other light as literature could shed if it were rightly studied."[3]

Foerster's insistence on the relevance of values in literary criticism was evident in the course entitled "Literature and the Art of Writing," which was a new title (as listed in the 1932–33 University *Catalogue*) for the two-year course required of all freshmen and sophomores. In a paper-bound handbook that was subsequently prepared, the intent of the course was explained in this way: "What is expected is that you will confront earnestly, with your whole nature, some of the central questions of human life as they have been represented in literature."[4]

In opposition to the scientific nature of philological investigation, Norman Foerster stood for a liberal foundation that precluded premature specialization at the undergraduate level. "We must aim," he wrote, "not at a merely factual, external accuracy but at a properly proportioned accuracy in facts, ideas, aesthetic perception, and taste in its full meaning."[5] Rejecting the predominating influence of German scholarship in favor of the French approach, Foerster professed the ideal of a well rounded education: "a scholarship at once scientific and critical, close to the facts but dominating them through general ideas, taste, and critical insight, contributing to knowledge in the best sense, and developing rather than warping the scholar himself."[6] One of Foerster's students later put it this way:

> Humanism to Babbitt and Foerster meant the intellectual dignity of man without a supernatural framework; in literature, it meant the ideas of a piece of writing, the ethos as opposed to the aesthetics. Explications, as Foerster encouraged them, were therefore chiefly concerned with the ideas; and insofar as they dealt with characters they dealt not with the psychological qualities of the person or his surrounding society and its influences, but rather the decisions he made on a set of judgments usually referred back to those other "humanists"—the Greeks of the great period.[7]

Foerster believed that "accuracy of this higher sort" could be encouraged by practice not only in historical and critical writing (or interpretive writing), but also in creative writing, which would "assist an inner comprehension of art."[8] At the time, neither area was a conventional pursuit for a scholar. As an incidental effect, Foerster hoped that by designing an academic program to serve the needs of creative writers the problem with their being so "lamentably uneducated" could in part be remedied. Later, when Foerster presented a list of recommendations from the School of Letters to the Iowa faculty of the College of Liberal Arts, one of the eight goals was merely a reiteration of this aspect of his approach:

> To provide a rigorous but liberalizing discipline in all the leading types of literary activity—the study of language, the study of literary history,

the study of literature as an art, literary criticism, and imaginative writing. Specialization, but not premature specialization, will be encouraged.[9]

It was in relation to creative writing and its rightful status within the academy that Norman Foerster's thought was truly revolutionary. This is not to say that the idea of learning through practice was a new one. At the University of Iowa, the principle had been invoked since the 1890s as justification for courses in creative writing. In 1922, Dean Carl Seashore had played an instrumental role in the decision by the Graduate College to grant the Master of Arts degree for creative work. And ten days before his death in 1939, Edwin Ford Piper wrote in a letter, "For forty years I have maintained that writing is as proper a field for the student as any other."[10] But it was Norman Foerster who persuaded the administration and the Board of Education to accept creative dissertations for the University's highest degree, the Doctor of Philosophy. In adopting Foerster's program, the University of Iowa became the first educational institution in America to permit submission of creative work for the doctoral dissertation as part of its regular curriculum.

Another one of Foerster's important contributions was his performance in the classroom. His teaching of "Literary Criticism" has been described by Iowa graduates as "extremely stimulating" and "the most personally significant course" encountered in graduate school.[11] Ruth V. Bortin, who was working on a book of verse for her master's thesis, felt that Foerster's course in criticism "opened entirely new fields" for her and she found it "intensely exciting":

> Like many of his students I regarded Dr. Foerster with something like idolatry. His courses were hard, he expected a large amount of background reading, but always stimulating. One of the courses I took with him was a seminar which met at his home. I remember being very impressed by the way he would refer to a book, then walk to the bookcase, which covered an entire wall of the study, and take down the book and refer to the quotation without the least fumbling or uncertainty.[12]

Wallace Stegner later observed that, "Foerster, though a New Humanist and very sure of his philosophical ground, was also intellectually open: We spent most of our time disagreeing with his positions and liking him personally."[13] Another of his students, Wilbur Schramm, described Foerster as "a man of elegant speech and manner, who read his lectures, then put them on reserve for students to read them again." Schramm recalled:

Foerster was . . . a challenge to students like Stegner and me, who had come out of greatly different backgrounds. We could learn the philology and the history easily; that required merely some careful reading and a good memory. But "Literary Criticism," which was Foerster's great course and the only course of his I can remember, was far from routine. It gave us a chance to live with the men who lived with ideas—Plato, Aristotle, Aquinas, and the like. We were challenged to face up to those ideas and bring our different wise men and our different worlds to test them. As I reflect back upon that time, it seems to me that another challenge Foerster presented us was a certain rigidity of mind and character that one might not have expected of a humanist: a firm sense of what was right and what was not, what was acceptable and what was not, usually measured on an inflexible model reaching from Aristotle to Babbitt. This quality led us to argue against his judgments, and to pit our more recent philosophical teachers against his classicists. Yet the experience was heavy and exciting, certainly the most modern and stimulating that Iowa had to offer graduate students in Letters at that time.

Schramm also observed that Foerster's "rigidity may have helped to explain later developments at Iowa," but maintained that "to students in the early 30s it was a challenge":

We had just come out of the 20's, a time we did not particularly respect. We felt we were in a new world, requiring new ideas and interpretations, new political leaders, new thinkers, new writers. It was a world of science and economics and psychology, and principles somewhat different from the ones that marched through Foerster's lectures. Therefore, we respected him and, I suppose, loved him, without agreeing with him. We found ourselves in the delightful position of working with a man who was so ideologically rigid that he forced us to have our own ideas in some kind of order, and yet permitted us to have our own heroes and speak for our own viewpoints.[14]

While the successes generally outweighed the failures in the first part of Norman Foerster's fourteen-year term at Iowa, his last years were marked by increasing opposition and controversy and by a final, humiliating setback in 1944 when the faculty voted to eliminate part of his program. According to Frances Mary Flanagan in her dissertation, "The Educational Role of Norman Foerster" (1971), Foerster's decision to resign his position at Iowa was the result of many factors, but the two most significant were an ideological confrontation with Dean Newburn over the curriculum and problems caused by Foerster's undefined bounds of authority as director of the School of Letters.[15]

From the beginning of Foerster's directorship, his new perspective and emphasis were met by a certain degree of opposition on the part of the more conservative members of the faculty, especially among the philologists and linguists. A long-standing ideological quarrel developed between Foerster and Professor Ernest Kuhl, who taught courses in Shakespeare and Chaucer. As the dispute intensified, Ernest Kuhl began writing angry letters protesting Foerster's policies to Baldwin Maxwell, head of the English Department, Dean Kay, President Jessup, and even Foerster himself. The dissension among the faculty soon became apparent to the graduate students, as evidenced by one student's recollection of the time:

> I don't really know how serious a cleavage there was between the English department and the School of Letters of which Foerster was Director. Among the graduate students it was supposed to exist and to be important in choosing a thesis topic, a faculty advisor, etc. It was supposed that Dr. Kuhl, with whom I had Chaucer, represented the traditionalists. I was personally distressed over the C I received in Chaucer, and at the time comforted by the idea that he didn't like students involved in creative writing. Looking back I think I probably got the grade I deserved.[16]

The animosity that developed between Foerster and Kuhl was so intensely felt that when Kuhl was interviewed in January 1977 at the age of ninety-five he criticized Foerster for not knowing Greek when his "Sermon on the Mount was the Greek civilization." Kuhl was quick to assert that when Foerster resigned "he hadn't a single friend on the faculty," though, he admitted that Foerster had retained a "certain following" among the students. Kuhl also noted that Hardin Craig (who founded the University's *Philological Quarterly* in 1922) had confided in him his disapprobation of Foerster's activities.

A major disappointment in Foerster's career was his failure to establish a journal distinctively identified with the thought and principles of the School of Letters. In 1935, *American Prefaces* was founded with Wilbur Schramm as editor and Foerster as an advisory editor. The journal was published for eight years under the auspices of the School of Letters with the support of the Graduate College, the School of Journalism, and the School of Fine Arts, but Foerster was never completely satisfied with the publication, in spite of its national prominence. Flanagan suggests that the reason was "probably because he saw that it might interfere with the development of the kind of journal that he longed to establish." The journal that Foerster had in mind, in Flanagan's view, "would represent the Humanist approach to literary studies, not being merely critical and imaginative like *American Prefaces*, not merely philological and historical, as *PQ* was meant to be, but providing a unified and total approach to literature."[17] Foerster's plan, then, was to recast the *Philological Quarterly* and to initiate the publication of a "journal of humane letters." When his proposal was rejected by the Graduate Council, it came as a bitter blow.[18]

There were other disappointments less serious in nature. In a letter to John Gerber, Foerster observed that C. A. Phillips, the acting president, "did not endear himself by refusing to allow me to bring Sinclair Lewis to help the Imaginative Writing students because he had, allegedly, once been intoxicated when lecturing in Cedar Rapids."[19] But the adoption of the Newburn curriculum was of far greater significance. Foerster equated Newburn's approach with "the specialist and vocational over-emphasis which has made liberal education impossible for the past quarter of a century."[20]

The stage was set for the crisis by a change in the University administration. In 1940, Virgil Hancher replaced Eugene Gilmore as president of the University and in 1941 Harry K. Newburn replaced George F. Kay as dean of the College of Liberal Arts. Prior to his appointment, Harry Newburn's experience had been limited almost entirely to the Department of Education. Foerster considered him an unenlightened Deweyite and a "progressive educationist."

Newburn's scientific orientation led him to devise a new approach to composition which he hoped would be "more readily amenable to measurement." His curricular "house-cleaning" involved early specialization, dropping the foreign language requirement, and an increased emphasis on basic skills in composition. The plan would separate the teaching of composition from the study of literature and would reduce the core requirement in literature from twelve to eight hours, thereby abandoning the two-year program developed earlier by Foerster.[21] As tempers heated in successive discussions and arguments, ideological positions were presented on an increasingly rhetorical level and in an increasingly personal tone, until Hancher and Foerster were finally drawn into an antagonistic position.

At the height of the debate, a group of graduate students in English circulated a petition expressing their "approval of the liberal educational ideals of the State University of Iowa" and declaring their support for Foerster, because he was "for the most part responsible for the creation and administration of this program." The petition continued:

> Specifically, we wish to state our approval of the graduate program in English. Many of us have been graduate students at other universities

and chose to come here because:

(1) It is possible to do a creative dissertation.

(2) There is an emphasis on ideas rather than linguistics and statistical research.

(3) There is an emphasis on the classics which does not exclude the serious consideration of twentieth-century writers.[22]

Following the formal adoption of the Newburn curriculum in April of 1944, Foerster exacerbated his already strained relations with Hancher by airing his grievances in letters to the local newspapers.

In spite of the official abandonment of his program, Norman Foerster did not commit himself to resignation until late in the summer of 1944. The deciding factor, according to Flanagan, was the lack of administrative support in delineating the bounds of his authority and in defending his right "to select and retain the kind of faculty his program demanded."[23] The problem was related to a flaw in the initial organization of the loosely structured School of Letters. Foerster was never sure of the extent of his control over department chairmen because his role as director had been defined in such sweeping terms: "the departments involved 'would continue to function as departments,' while 'the common areas of study would be fostered and developed in all their aspects.' "[24] When he learned that a man in his own department had been promoted to a permanent position not only without his recommendation but without his knowledge, Foerster, deciding that his position had become entirely untenable, submitted his resignation and returned to Chapel Hill.[25]

In retrospect, the nature and extent of Foerster's reaction to the Newburn proposal might seem extreme, but only to someone who did not know him. Wilbur Schramm pointed out:

> He could have argued his case and accepted the faculty decision. He could have gone along with the university decision and still maintained higher requirements for the Department of English or the School of Letters. But by some mechanism or other, he interpreted this faculty decision as an all or none matter. Like so many other things he had taught us, a decision of this kind was either right or wrong, and this one seemed to him very wrong. He put himself on the line—this decision or me.

Schramm was also aware of a certain "rigidity" on the part of "some of his close associates in the Department," a factor which Schramm felt "must have strengthened him in his perception of the decision as the whole war, rather than a battle within a continuing struggle." Furthermore, he speculated that Foerster could have been "feeling a bit lonely at that time, a bit deserted by the persons he had thought of as his 'humanist' allies." In any case, the controversy surrounding the decision led to a falling out between Foerster and Schramm, though Schramm denies that there was ever a total break in their previously close relationship:

> I did not agree with him, and told him so. He reacted with a great coldness, which grieved me, and I was never so close to him again. The faculty decision went against him, and he returned to his home, spending most or all of his time there, and soon resigning his Professorship and Directorship.[26]

While serving on the Iowa faculty, Norman Foerster—Ernest Kuhl's pronouncement notwithstanding—established a number of deep and lasting friendships among his colleagues. Paul Engle wrote to Foerster in regard to his resignation:

> It has been my privilege to tell both Dean Newburn and President Hancher my opinion that anything which caused you to leave the university would be most deplorable, and that as far as I myself was concerned, I felt your presence here was a strength to the university as a whole, and a needed support for the writing program. I want you to know I said that, and I want it down on paper. As you probably know, I did not feel as strongly as you last spring that the new curriculum would devastate us. But I did feel that your being here was important beyond any curricular change. It is right that I have said that to the administration (to Pres. Hancher the same day I came to your house). I wish you might have stayed. After all, I would not be here without the position you created more or less for me, and I appreciate that. While differing often, it has always been a solid pleasure to know that I could walk into your office and discuss anything without restraint. The attitude which you represent in the university is one I hate to see go, for we have enough of what might be called the "scientific" mind, and a humane leavening of the right kind of scholarship is indispensable. The modifications in the direction of flexibility and value which you brought to graduate study were admirable in the extreme, and I worry that they shall be lost, and that we will return to what is cruelly called "real scholarship."[27]

To assess Norman Foerster's role in the founding of the Writers' Workshop is to speak of a two-fold contribution. He once referred to the Ph.D. in imaginative writing as the English Department's "widest departure from convention."[28] The fact that he was the man primarily responsible for the success of this experiment is undeniable. His work to make the creative Ph.D. academically respectable was crucial. But the question remains:

Would the Writers' Workshop have been established at the University of Iowa without the contribution and influence of Norman Foerster?

Taking into account the cumulative efforts of many individuals and the momentum that had preceded Foerster's term at Iowa, it seems likely enough that the Writers' Workshop would have been established, although perhaps not for some time. On the other hand, there is the question of how much weight should be given to Frederick's assessment that by 1928 the Department of English was moving in the direction of scholarly research and abandoning the direction of "unique distinction" that previously had characterized the program. If Frederick's warning was not unwarranted, then it is apparent that Foerster's counter-balancing role was vital to the expansion of creative endeavor and that without his influence the Writers' Workshop might never have developed at the University of Iowa—or at least not until the idea had been proven elsewhere and it had become fashionable for universities and colleges to organize their own workshops, as happened in the sixties.

The second area of Foerster's contribution has to do with the nature of the program that did in fact develop. Here, the extent of his influence can be discerned with greater decision. Just as his new humanist perspective lent a national orientation to the 1931 Conference on Creative Writing and could be seen as well in the relative absence of local flavor in *American Prefaces*, so Foerster transformed the developing program in creative writing from a regional to a national institution. The result was clear: Iowa City continued to grow as a center for creative writing—as the regionalists had hoped it would—but the old regionalist spirit was superseded by a new attention to national concerns and literary trends.

NOTES

1 Norman Foerster, *The American Scholar* (Chapel Hill: University of North Carolina Press, 1929), pp. 13–14.

2 *Ibid.*, pp. 13, 18.

3 *Ibid.*, p. 42.

4 Foerster, *Literature and the Art of Writing* (Iowa City: State University of Iowa, 1936–37), p. 15.

5 Foerster, *The American Scholar*, p. 60.

6 *Ibid.*, p. 61.

7   Wilbur Schramm, letter to the author, "Workshop Correspondence with Wilbers," no. 251, University of Iowa Archives, Iowa City.

8   Foerster, *The American Scholar*, p. 60.

9   Foerster, "Recommendations to the Faculty of the College of Liberal Arts from the School of Letters," February 26, 1931, Norman Foerster Papers, University of Iowa Archives, Iowa City.

10   Edwin Ford Piper, letter to Professor Bishop, May 7, 1939, Edwin Ford Piper Papers, University of Iowa Archives, Iowa City.

11   Wallace Stegner, letter to the author, February 26, 1976, "Workshop Correspondence with Wilbers," no. 41, University of Iowa Archives, Iowa City.

12   Ruth V. Bortin, letter to the author, April 21, 1976, no. 113, University of Iowa Archives, Iowa City.

13   Stegner, letter to the author, no. 41.

14   Wilbur Schramm, letter to the author, no. 251.

15   Frances Mary Flanagan, "The Educational Role of Norman Foerster," Ph.D. dissertation, University of Iowa, 1971, pp. 140, 249.

16   Bortin, letter to the author, no. 113.

17   Flanagan, p. 154.

18   *Ibid.*, pp. 154ff.

19   Foerster, letter to Gerber, November 22, 1971, University of Iowa Archives, Iowa City. In a letter from Phillips to Foerster (dated August 30, 1940, and stored in the Foerster Papers), however, Phillips seems merely to be relaying the decision of the Iowa State Board of Education.

20   Foerster, "Steps Toward Liberal Education, Steps Away From Liberal Education," an undated memorandum, Foerster Papers, University of Iowa Archives, Iowa City.

21   Flanagan, pp. 195ff.

22   Petition, March 20, 1944, Foerster Papers, University of Iowa Archives, Iowa City.

23   Flanagan, p. 249.

24   *Ibid.*, pp. 137, 140.

25   *Ibid.*, p. 150.

26   Schramm, letter to the author, no. 251.

27   Paul Engle, letter to Norman Foerster, August 8, 1944, Foerster Papers, University of Iowa Archives, Iowa City.

28   Foerster, memorandum to George F. Kay and George Stoddard, July 20, 1937, Foerster Papers, University of Iowa Archives, Iowa City.

III
GROWTH AND
CONSOLIDATION

Profile of Paul Engle

MORE THAN ANYONE else, Paul Engle deserves credit for making the Iowa Writers' Workshop the kind of program it is today and for establishing its reputation as the best writing program in the country. As Wilbur Schramm aptly observed, "My job was perhaps to preside at the birth, but Paul raised the infant."[1] A complex man whose vision and knack for obtaining publicity emanate from an egocentric genius, Paul Engle has shown himself to be a determined administrator and indefatigable worker. His incessant search for talented students and faculty, his remarkable success at fund-raising, his ability to draw national attention to the Workshop, his teaching and service to students, and perhaps above all his sheer energy combined to help produce a program that became an institution in American letters. During Paul Engle's twenty-four-year term as director, the Writers' Workshop grew from a dormant program that included fewer than a dozen students during the war years to one whose enrollment reached 250 graduate students in 1965.

Paul Engle's argument in support of the Program in Creative Writing was an extension of Norman Foerster's and Wilbur Schramm's line of thinking. Although the emphasis of the program under Engle's direction changed from treating creative writing as a part of a broader scholarly discipline to viewing scholarship as an activity beneficial to the writer, at base the premise was the same: the creation of literature is academically as respectable and important as the study of literature. Along with this went the conviction that the Ph.D. in imaginative writing should differ from the conventional Ph.D. only in regard to the dissertation. Otherwise, imaginative writers seeking the degree were required to satisfy all the conditions set for the degree, including minimum hours of coursework, distribution requirements, and comprehensive examinations.

Among his many articles on the subject, Engle's introduction to *Midland, An Anthology of Poetry and Prose* (1961) provides his most complete statement. The introduction, entitled "The Writer and the Place," opens with a description of what Engle called an "institutional vision":

This book is the result of a vision.

By vision, I do not mean the abrupt and ecstatic experience of Saul on the road to Damascus, blinded by a light "above the brightness of the sun," and startled by a voice speaking from heaven.

By vision, I mean the steady development at the University of Iowa of the conviction that the creative imagination in all of the arts is as important, as congenial, and as necessary, as the historical study of all the arts. How simple, and yet how reckless.

This gradual revelation was quite as astonishing as a sudden idea seen, for the first time, in a flash of light. It took imagination, some years ago, for an educational institution to put its trust in the imaginative arts. Logical as the theory that it is as proper to encourage the writing of a good poem as the study of a bad one (or even of a good one) might sound, what would really happen when the poets arrived? Were they not traditionally doubtful types, likely to turn up wearing a nest of robins in their hair?

Universities are not famous for taking chances, but the University of Iowa took one.[2]

Basically, the question asked by Engle was, "If the mind could be honored . . . [in the university], why not the imagination?" It was the same question asked by Norman Foerster and others before him.

In support of this argument, Engle likened the teaching that can be done in a workshop to the function of an editor like Maxwell Perkins, who shaped and pared into presentable form the massive manuscripts of Thomas Wolfe. He drew an analogy between the student enrolling in a workshop and the artist seeking instruction by a master, and spoke of criticism's maturing influence on the writer's attitude toward his work:

> After all, has the painter not always gone to an art school, or at least to an established master, for instruction? And the composer, the sculptor, the architect? Then why not the writer? Good poets, like good hybrid corn, are both born and made. Right criticism can speed up the maturing of a poet by years. More than that, tough and detailed criticism of a young writer can help him become his own shrewd critic so that, when he publishes, the critics will not have to be tough on him.[3]

In Engle's discussion of "The Writer and the Place," the "Place" referred to was the university in American society, and more specifically, the University of Iowa in Iowa City. His argument for establishing a regional center in the Midwest, strongly reminiscent of John T. Frederick's declaration in the *Midland*'s first issue, was presented in this way:

In a country with so ranging a landscape, with its concentrations of culture so widely diffused, the problem of where a young writer is to feel at home becomes far more urgent than in England, where London is in easy reach. There must be an alternative between Hollywood and New York, between those places psychically as well as geographically. The University of Iowa tries to offer such a community, congenial to the young writer, with his uneasiness about writing as an honorable career, or with his excess of ego about calling himself a writer. To them, we offer hard criticism and decent sympathy. More than that, our way of mimeographing poetry and fiction for the Workshops offers everyone a hearing. To have your work read by all of the members of the Workshop, and publicly criticized and praised by your instructors in the weekly meetings, represents a helpful and at the same time less hazardous form of publication.

The system offers proof that writing can be seriously regarded, and that it is a difficult art not only worth an absolute commitment of faith, time and energy, but demanding it. The writer finds that the students around him are alert to his faults and quick to praise his virtues. In brief, he is, while practicing a completely private art, reassured by a sense of belonging to a group which gives him a decent regard. For as long as he is a part of this community, he has a useful competition with those around him, and at the same time is freed from the imperatives of a market place, as he may never be again. He can have a manner of publication without losing too much blood.[4]

On the other hand, Engle—like Norman Foerster and Wilbur Schramm—was careful to delineate the limits to what the university could do for the writer:

We do not pretend to have produced the writers included in this book. Their talent was inevitably shaped by the genes rattling in the ancestral closets. We did give them a community in which to try out the quality of their gift, as New Englanders used to speak of trying out the oil from whale blubber. Much of this writing was done in Iowa City and received our criticism. Some of it was written far away. In either case, the writer was for a while part of the community we have made here where the University has stood in the position of friend and, to a slighter degree than we would wish, of patron.[5]

This "matter of place," as Engle called it, was at the heart of both the regionalist movement and the artistic community in general.

Unlike the regionalists before him, Engle was not motivated by a desire to make Iowa City a midwestern cultural center. Instead, his ambition, as revealed in a letter to President Hancher in 1963, was "to run the future of

American literature, and a great deal of European and Asian, through Iowa City." And, he reported, "We are on the way."[6] Though himself an Iowan who was appreciative of his local culture, Engle rejected the thrust of the regionalist movement:

> I have the warmest feeling for the Midwest and have written much about it, but the Workshop had to strive for excellence, not localism. I always felt that Grant Wood was too assertively "Iowan," especially since he learned his stylizing technique not here but in Munich and especially the Pieter Breughel the Elder paintings in the Alte Pinakotek, and in Paris studios.[7]

A closer look at Paul Engle, his background and motivating concerns, will help explain why his attention was drawn to a larger stage.

Born in 1908 and raised in Cedar Rapids (twenty-four miles from Iowa City), Paul Engle seemed driven by a desire to excel from an early age. His environment proved a stimulating one, with a number of benefactors encouraging him to write. When he showed his first poems (a sequence of Shakespearean sonnets) to Elizabeth Cock, a high school teacher who conducted poetry sessions after class, she took a special interest in him and began giving him books. Later, Gabriel Newburger, the son of immigrant peddlars from Vienna, and Luther Brewer, a devotee of Leigh Hunt, became influential figures in Engle's development, as did Jay Sigmund, a local insurance salesman who introduced him to the poetry of Charles Baudelaire, Conrad Aiken, and Arthur Rimbaud. In addition to working a paper route, helping his father train horses, and gardening, Paul Engle worked afternoons and evenings at East End Pharmacy, where Art Clark, another benefactor, ordered literary magazines like the *Little Review* and *Transition* for him to read at work, despite the fact that these magazines rarely sold. He attended Washington High School, where he was chosen class poet.

As a student at Coe College, Paul Engle considered studying for the Methodist ministry and even preached at Stumptown church on the edge of Cedar Rapids. But, in his own words, "I heard no call." Abandoning the ministry in favor of geology, he began collecting fossils from the Devonian limestone which underlies the cornfields of eastern Iowa. At the University of Iowa, he decided on a career in literature.

After a Lydia Roberts Fellowship for students from Iowa enabled him to go to Columbia University for a year of graduate study in both anthropology and literature, a Rhodes Scholarship took him to Merton College at Oxford, where he made the acquaintance of W. H. Auden and Stephen Spender and formed a lasting friendship with his tutor, Edmund Blunden. In 1934, his second collection of poems, *American Song*, was enthusiastically reviewed by J. Donald Adams on the front page of the *New York Times Book Review*. While in England, Engle played wicket keeper on the college cricket team and rowed in the College Eights, winning in his last year an oar in the College First Eight and competing in the International Regattas at Marlowe and Henley-on-Thames. Before joining the University of Iowa faculty as a lecturer in poetry in 1937, Engle travelled extensively on the Continent, then travelled for a year across the United States and lectured on modern literature and the nature of poetry. This breadth of experience prior to the period of his directorship was undoubtedly a factor in his concern for both the national and the international literary scenes.

In reviewing the events of his boyhood and his affiliation with the University of Iowa, Paul Engle observed jokingly in an interview, "There are few people who have remained neutral in regard to my life. Some like me excessively, feel a great affection for me, and some dislike me excessively, hate my guts. I probably don't deserve either extreme." He attributed this sharply divided response to his double nature, which he believes he inherited from his mother and father:

> I regard myself as being split, not in a medical sense, not meaning in a psychically ill sense of the word (although you could get a few who would support that view too), but split between these two forces within me. As I look back on my career, I can see that I was an odd combination—in about equal parts—of my mother and of my father, who were absolute opposites in human personality.[8]

From his mother, whom he described as a brilliant but very gentle and soft-spoken person, he inherited his more sensitive and imaginative nature. From his father, whose business was horses—race horses, carriage horses, work horses, and saddle horses which his father bought, sold, trained, and rented—he acquired his drive. He described his father as "a tough, driving, hard-working man":

> He never even finished eighth grade in a country school, but he was bright and people liked him. And if you deal with horses the way he did—training them and breaking them—it takes a certain amount of strength and determination as well as skill. My father would comment on the weather as if he was challenging you to step outside.

John Engels (who attended the Workshop in 1956–57) has offered this portrait of Engle's complex nature:

> Paul Engle was the dominant figure in the workshops. He was charming, difficult, cantankerous, demanding, generous, cold and reserved, warm and open, a man of so many contradictions it would be presumptuous of me to attempt to resolve them. To me he was

always kind. He made it possible, economically, for me to stay on at Iowa with an unofficial grant. He made it possible for me to attend in the first place, on very little evidence of talent. The workshops could not have existed without him, nor remained in existence. He traveled a great deal, worked at outside projects, often seemed distracted by demands apart from the workshops, and was criticized for this. He responded strongly to people, and there were powerful tensions between him and his faculty; but of these I had no first-hand knowledge. The faculty had a tendency to enlist students in their causes, and armies arose, always for or against Engle who attracted everybody's lightning, as I suppose was inevitable. I liked him, was and am grateful to him, feared him, was dependent on him critically and in other ways I no longer understand. My feelings were not, and are not, shared by everyone I knew at Iowa.[9]

Possessed by a sense of urgency, Engle was convinced that "mediocrity triumphs" in too many cases. "You do not create new programs without driving hard and if you drive hard you're going to irritate people," he later explained in an interview. "Quiet people don't offend." Engle attributes his success in garnering support for the Program in Creative Writing both to the quality of the students and to his unique policy of "delicate and imaginative aggression." To illustrate this, he offered the following anecdote:

You know, in order to survive in the academic world, you have to learn very quickly to perceive which person is likely to be for you and which person is likely not to be. I soon discovered that [former Provost] Harvey Davis was the kind of person who believed in hard evidence and was very interested in what I was trying to do. I'll never forget the time I staggered into his office and emptied the contents of two suitcases onto his desk and said, "I thought it might interest you to know that my people are not simply writing manuscripts for a class. They are publishing books and here are their books of the last few years." Well, all administrators believe in publication, you know. So he said, "Yes, I'm delighted to find that your people are very productive. And now I see the point in your coming here with them. Just what do you want?" And I said, "We need space."

At the time, the Workshop was crowded into a single temporary barrack located north of the Iowa Memorial Union. In a short while, three additional barracks were made available to the program.

Much of the program's success was due to Engle's personal commitment, which drove him to great lengths in his search for talent, outside contributions, and publicity. Once convinced of a student's potential,

Engle would provide the kind of support he himself had received as a youth. One example of this is the case of Charles Embree (a member of the Workshop, on and off, from 1946 to 1952), who was impressed by Engle's way of sizing up young people and by his willingness to speculate on talent:

Actually, at this time, my membership in the Workshop was unofficial. I had come to the University with no writing experience—the previous four years had been spent in the Navy as an artist—so Engle had no basis for allowing me to enroll in his class. He did permit me to audit it. One day I ran into him on campus and he asked me if I had yet written a story. I had, indeed—my very first one—and by chance I had it with me. He took it with him. A few days later he asked me to read it in class—apparently having forgotten that I wasn't a member. I didn't remind him. I went ahead and read the story. To my surprise, it made a hit. Secretly, Engle sent it to *Esquire.* Secretly, they bought it. At the next meeting of the class Engle dropped the bomb. It was a real shocker for everyone but especially for me. Before I could recover my wits, Engle adjourned the class and we celebrated the event at the Airliner, a beer joint across the street—at my expense, of course. I think this was the first sale of a short story to a major magazine by a Workshop member, even an unofficial one. Anyhow, it was a joyous occasion created by and made memorable by Paul Engle. That's the kind of teacher he was, that's the way the Workshop worked.[10]

Some of Engle's controversial decisions as an administrator are more easily understood when viewed in relation to his goal of making Iowa City a world center for writers. The only program worth running, in his opinion, was the best one. But acting on this conviction sometimes caused problems. In reference to the English Department's opposition to his dismissing a Workshop instructor, Engle has written:

The profound point in all this controversy was that at no time did any of the others mention either the future good of the Workshop or the University, only the rights of colleagues regarded quite without the slightest care for the intense struggle I had carried on for years to build a nationally distinguished Workshop on a pitiful financial base. Forty years of observation of University faculties, including Harvard and LSU, where I taught, and many others where I lectured, have convinced me that too many faculty members look at teaching as a priesthood, from which one cannot be terminated save for the grossest (and public) moral scandal (if it can be kept secret, as has happened here, no problem). The idea of a colleague simply drifting along in idleness, non-productivity, and continuing acts of public drunkenness is acceptable. Leap to his defense, without regard to the future excellence of the University. It is my firm conviction that too few faculty members are fired. Produce or get out, and the old bromide that "he doesn't do books but he's a fine teacher" I believe to be wrong. The best teachers I had were the most productive. I have listened to the spoken (and read the written, little as it was) English of such people and can't believe those voices could effectively instruct the young.[11]

It was Engle's belief that only practicing and publishing writers should teach in the Workshop and it was a principle on which he was unwilling to compromise.

In assessing Paul Engle's term as director of the Writers' Workshop, it could be argued that his greatest strength was also his greatest weakness. While his remarkable drive and determination were the key to his effectiveness in expanding the program, these same qualities offended those who viewed his efforts as self-serving. Moreover, they left him vulnerable to attack from those who resented his accomplishments. Although most of his years as director were without controversy, some hostility between the writers and the scholars of the department preceded and continued throughout his term. Perhaps the secret to both his success and his ability to offend lay in his uncompromising insistence on running nothing less than a first-rate program—first-rate at whatever cost, whether that involved personal sacrifice, time taken from his own writing, or hard-nosed decisions regarding the hiring and firing and general handling of his faculty. In this way, his sense of urgency and his outright impatience in accomplishing his goals were both valuable and costly.

NOTES

1   Wilbur Schramm in a letter to Jean Wylder, February 14, 1973, copy in "Workshop Correspondence with Wilbers," no. 225, University of Iowa Archives, Iowa City.

2   Paul Engle, "Introduction: The Writer and the Place," *Midland, An Anthology of Poetry and Prose,* edited by Paul Engle with assistance from Henri Coulette and Donald Justice (New York: Random House, 1961), p. xxi. On page xxxiv, Engle credits the following people:

> . . . it was a Swedish immigrant, Carl E. Seashore, who became interested in locating creative talent on this campus. As Dean of the Graduate College, he was the first person in the United States to print in an academic catalogue the startling news that creative work was to be considered as acceptable for

advanced degrees. The view that imaginative writing was an honorable activity of the total man, involving his intelligence as well as his sympathetic nervous system, was continued by George D. Stoddard while Dean of the Graduate College (Dr. Stoddard is now Chancellor of New York University), and Norman Foerster, while Director of the School of Letters here; the late Dean Walter F. Loehwing, scientist, was a steady support. Ted McCarrel, Registrar, took bold chances by admitting many writing students with the most melodramatic academic records. Loren Hickerson, Alumni Director, Philip Kruidenier and the State University of Iowa Foundation have been a pillar of cloud by day. James R. Jordan, Gordon Strayer and Ken Donelson, of University Relations, have been a pillar of flame by night.

3 *Ibid.,* p. xxiv.

4 *Ibid.,* pp. xxv–xxvi.

5 *Ibid.,* p. xxx.

6 Engle in a letter to Virgil Hancher, October 31, 1963, copy in "Writers' Workshop," University of Iowa Archives, Iowa City.

7 Quoted from Engle's written response to the first draft of the chapter on the "Engle Workshop," University of Iowa Archives, Iowa City.

8 Charles Embree, letter to the author, March 11, 1976, "Workshop Correspondence with Wilbers," no. 73, University of Iowa Archives, Iowa City. The following letter gives an indication of the lengths Engle would go to in order to help a promising writer:

Dear Mr. _____:
    I hope you will forgive a complete stranger writing you about a member of your own family. _____ _____ has come here to complete his work for the B.A. degree with an emphasis on writing. As you know, his record during his previous college attempt was not very good. However, I am convinced that he is determined to do well here, and, of course, he is quite capable of surpassing the great bulk of students. He has taken entrance examinations here and on the important ones scored 94 and 91, which is in the top 3%, a very remarkable effort. The problem is to motivate him to use the excellent mind that he has. I am sure that he will use it here, and that he will not only do his degree, but do it superbly well. He already has taken a job working 80 hours a month in addition to a full schedule of classes he contemplates. If he does as well as I expect him to this first semester, I hope to get him a scholarship for the second.
    My reason for writing you is this—he must, before he can even register for classes, pay his entrance fee of $100. After that he will have tuition and fees, about $212. If he could receive from you, by telegram the $100, if not the total amount, he could at least begin his work, while we attempted to find the balance by loan. I realize that you may have personal reservations about helping _____ again, but it seems to me that there is one very crucial reason why you should do so now—this is the big step forward in _____'s career. He wants to settle down to work. He will do so if the University is available to him. If he can complete his degree, it will make his whole career alter for the better. If, however, he should not be able to, but has to leave and take any sort of job, it may well be the last chance he will have to bring his life together in a shape and an order.

_____ has a deep and genuine talent. He can become, with a year's encouragement and security, one of this country's finest young poets, a public credit to you as his father and a valuable addition to the culture of the country as a whole. If he did not have such talent, I would not take time from my own work to attempt to help him along. Let me say that I have devoted many hours in the past two days in interceding for _____, to finding ways to help, and to securing him the last, final chance he needs.

In my mind, there is no risk at all in predicting that, if given the opportunity, your son will earn a distinguished year at this University. Whatever investment you may feel it possible to make in his future will be proved right and good. I have talked with him at length several times, and am perfectly aware that he has had his problems in the past. This is it. He can triumph over them, with your aid. If you could feel that it was suitable to wire him the money for his entrance fee and/or tuition, for this one semester only, you would have my gratitude as well as his, and the satisfaction of locating _____ in a place where he can get his life and his talent organized . . . .

As a result of this effort, the young man's father, incensed by what he considered an outsider's interference, called Engle on the phone late one night and expressed his outrage in no uncertain terms, but after a long discussion he was persuaded to view Engle's interest in his son as a token of esteem. The money was finally sent, the young man completed his studies successfully, and then went on to become one of the founding editors of a major poetry magazine.

9   The interview from which this excerpt is taken appeared as part of an article in the *Iowa Alumni Review*, 30 (June/July 1977), 8–13.

10   John Engels, letter to the author, February 17, 1976, "Workshop Correspondence with Wilbers," no. 12, University of Iowa Archives, Iowa City.

11   Quoted from Engle's written response to the first draft of the chapter on the "Engle Workshop," University of Iowa Archives, Iowa City.

The Engle Workshop

AT THE BEGINNING of Paul Engle's term as director of the Writers' Workshop, it was becoming more and more common for America's well known writers to seek teaching positions within universities and for the universities to include writers as part of their faculties. While the advent of World War II caused a general reduction in activities on most American campuses, it did not interfere with this change, which had been taking place on the American literary scene since the mid-thirties, a change that had been effected at least in part by the Iowa example. This new attitude seemed to manifest itself even more strongly during the postwar years.

As Wallace Stegner noted in "New Climates for the Writer" (one of a series of lectures on the writer in America that he gave in Japan in 1951), new writers were becoming increasingly a product of the universities, and established writers were looking increasingly to the universities for sanctuary. In support of this contention, Stegner listed these writer-teachers: Robert Penn Warren at Minnesota, Saul Bellow formerly at Minnesota, Robert Frost at Dartmouth, Paul Engle and Ray West at Iowa, Maxwell Geismar at Sara Lawrence, Theodore Morrison, John Ciardi and Albert Guerard at Harvard, Mary McCarthy at Bard College, George R. Stewart and Mark Shorer at California, Allen Tate and Caroline Gordon formerly at Princeton and more recently at a series of colleges, John Crowe Ransom at Kenyon College, Donald Davidson at Vanderbilt, Hudson Strode at Alabama, Delmore Schwartz and John Berryman formerly at Harvard, Cleanth Brooks at Louisiana State, Arthur Mizener at Carleton College, Yvor Winters, Richard Scowcroft, and Stegner himself at Stanford. Stegner went on to point out that a growing number of literary publications and collections like Martha Foley's *The Best American Short Stories* and Herschel Brickell's *Prize Stories* were dominated by "academic" writers.[1]

At the University of Iowa as elsewhere, the success of both students and faculty in publishing attracted more talented students, who in turn published and attracted more prominent faculty, who in turn attracted more talented writers. The 1950s were, in a sense, the decade during which the

Iowa Writers' Workshop consolidated its national reputation. The first real breakthrough in publicity occurred in February of 1952, when *Poetry* magazine devoted half of a special issue to poetry written by Iowa Workshop writers.[2] (The University of Washington's Poetry Workshop, under the direction of Theodore Roethke, supplied the poetry for the other half.) By 1953, six novels by Iowa Workshop students and graduates had either been published or accepted for publication during the preceding year. They included: Gene Brown's *Trespass* (Doubleday Doran), Flannery O'Connor's *Wise Blood* (Harcourt Brace), Oakley Hall's *Corpus of Joe Bailey* (Viking), Rocco Fumento's *Devil by the Tail* (McGraw-Hill), and Delmar Jackson's *The Cut of the Axe* (Harcourt Brace).

The academic year 1956–57—the year of Iowa's celebration in honor of Baudelaire and the first issue of the locally published literary magazine, *December*—was described by Workshop instructor Marguerite Young as the most successful year to date for fiction writers. Publications included short stories by Damon Swanson, John Gardner, and Tom Williams—as well as stories by members of the staff—in *Harper's Bazaar, Antioch Review, Botteghe Oscure,* and *Esquire.* That same year poems by Robert Mezey, Henri Coulette, Theodore Holmes, Paul Petrie, William Murray, Robert Sward, Philip Levine, and Knute Skinner appeared in the *Paris Review, Botteghe Oscure, Kenyon Review,* the *New Yorker, Accent, New Orleans Poetry Journal,* and *Poetry.*

In 1958, one-third of all contributors in the American section of the volume, *The New Poets of England and America,* were Iowa Workshop students or graduates. In that same year a number of poems and a short story appeared in *New Campus Writing No. 2,* which were written by workshop members. In 1959, the year that Iowa hosted the *Esquire* symposium, Donald Justice's first volume of poetry, *The Summer Anniversaries,* was chosen as the Lamont Poetry Selection by the Academy of American Poets, and William Dickey won the Yale Series of Younger Poets Award. In 1960, W. D. Snodgrass's *Heart's Needle* won the Pulitzer Prize in Poetry and Robert Mezey's *The Lovemaker* was the Lamont Poetry Selection.

During this period of consolidation, students at the Writers' Workshop tended to be older and more experienced than today's students, who are more likely to come directly from college to the graduate Workshop. As a result of the G.I. Bill, the student body was predominantly male, although the star student of the period was Flannery O'Connor. (Recipient of a fellowship from Rinehart & Company in 1947, O'Connor succeeded in publishing two short stories from her M.F.A. thesis in well respected literary magazines and was then at work on *Wise Blood*).[3]

Throughout the fifties, the atmosphere in both the Fiction and Poetry Workshops was personal, and for the most part easy-going and relaxed.

Paul Engle (right), second director of the Workshop, with guest Robert Frost at a reading for students and faculty in the "barracks," the temporary building north of the Iowa Memorial Union which housed the Workshop for nearly two decades.

The program was housed in plain, corrugated iron barracks that were constructed just after the war to accommodate the new influx of students. (Despite their having a useful life expectancy of only five years, the temporary barracks were used by the Workshop until 1966.) In addition, Paul Engle always seemed to be finding ways to supplement financial awards by providing discarded clothing, making arrangements for housing, getting babies delivered free, and even providing the baby crib. Often he would invite his students to his summer home in Stone City for a workshop or a party. His first wife, Mary Nissen Engle, went out of her way to be kind and helpful to their guests. She would usually accompany Paul to the bus stop or railroad station when he went to meet the new writers, and many times at midnight or one o'clock in the morning she would feed the new arrivals and put them up.

Because of the proximity in age between the students and faculty and owing to the ambience generated by the predominantly male group, a spirit of friendliness and camaraderie characterized student-faculty relations. Vance Bourjaily, who joined the Workshop faculty in 1957, later described this period when the program was smaller as a "more innocent time":

The Workshop itself was located in the temporary buildings over by the Union, which is now the Union parking lot, and I think we all had considerable affection for those old tin buildings. In 1957, there were still a number of older students around, the Korean War veterans, and it was in general a much younger faculty. We were all pretty close to the students in age. It made for an easy-going kind of student-teacher relationship. Tom Williams, whose book won the National Book Award last year, was a student here then. Tom was a guy who had published a novel before coming here and he was virtually my age—a couple years younger. Tom and I became very close friends and still are. We used to go duck hunting on the Iowa River together, morning after morning. Fishing in the spring. Our trout group would go to Northeast Iowa when spring came and would generally include Kim Merker, and a guy named Pete Everwine, a poet of some distinction now. In addition to hunting and fishing and the usual partying, there was a regular Friday night poker game that generally met at my house, which was again Merker, and Everwine, Tom Williams, Justice. Bill Murray used to play with us—he was a graduate student then. We all used to really look forward to our weekly poker game.[4]

In the late forties, the Workshop faculty included Hansford ("Mike") Martin, Paul Griffith, Andrew Lytle, and William Porter (who taught a course in magazine writing that was cross-listed in both the Workshop and the School of Journalism). In the early fifties, Martin continued to teach and R. V. Cassill and Ray B. West, Jr., (both Iowa graduates) joined the faculty. Others included Robert Lowell, Warren Carrier, John Berryman, Walter Van Tilburg Clark, and Thomas Mabry. And in the mid to late fifties, the faculty was at various times composed of Marguerite Young, Robert Bowen, Donald Justice, Vance Bourjaily, Harvey Swados, Curtis Harnack, Hortense Calisher, Bienvenido Santos, and George P. Elliott. By the end of the decade, the ranking faculty members were Paul Engle, Vance Bourjaily, Donald Justice, and Ray B. West.

In November 1959 the underground movement in Iowa City was given impetus by the opening of a coffee house called Renaissance II and by the appearance of a weekly newspaper called the *Iowa Defender* (or the *ID* which was meant to be, quite literally, an alternative publication to the *DI* or *Daily Iowan*). John Beardsley's coffee house (which ran from November 1959 until May 1960) featured a hi-fi room where customers could listen to their own records, a free expression room with walls covered with "witticisms," jazz concerts, and poetry readings. The *Iowa Defender* was first edited by Stephen Tudor, who had resigned his editorship of the *Daily Iowan* in protest against faculty censorship, and after the eighth issue was published by Gerald Stevenson, proprietor of the Qara Press and the Paper

Place bookstore. It appeared every Monday during the school year from 1959 to 1969, with the exception of 1966. The newspaper leaned toward the left politically, although it also served as a forum for a variety of views, and printed the poetry of resident poets like Marvin Bell, Jon Silkin, Michael Dennis Browne, James Tate, John O'Hara, Darrell Gray, and Ted Berrigan.[5]

During Paul Engle's tenure, the most significant additions to the curriculum of the Writers' Workshop occurred in the years 1949, 1957, and 1963. To accommodate the expanding enrollment of the postwar period, Engle divided the Workshop into the Poetry Workshop and the Fiction Workshop and reinstated (and for a while taught) the previously offered undergraduate courses in the understanding, appreciation, and practice of poetry and fiction. In 1949, there appeared for the first time in the University *Catalogue* the "Undergraduate Writers' Workshop," which was designed for "undergraduates other than freshmen interested in imaginative writing."[6] Nineteen forty-nine was also the first year that the Department of English offered an "English Major with emphasis on Creative Writing."

The next innovation in curriculum occurred in 1957. Acting on the conviction that many graduate students were handicapped in their attempts at creative writing by a poor background in literature, Engle instituted advanced courses in "Form and Theory of Fiction" (which in the first semester dealt with "predominant techniques in the modern short story" and in the second semester with "predominant techniques in the modern novel"), as well as advanced seminars in "Problems in Modern Poetry" and "Contemporary Authors."[7] In the spring semester of 1963, the "Translation Workshop" was begun. The rationale for the new workshop was to remedy American ignorance of contemporary foreign writers by providing English translations of their works.[8]

The heart of the program was of course the "workshops" themselves. These involved small groups of students meeting weekly with an instructor, discussing the work submitted, and offering suggestions to each other on how to improve it. Sometimes the instructors would combine their classes, which allowed them maximum contact with the greatest number of students. The student manuscripts were mimeographed and distributed on "worksheets" so that they could be read in advance and covered thoroughly in class. As Engle later described it, the faculty viewed the teaching at the Workshop as a shared experience:

> We [the faculty] would all read the poems and short stories and then meet an hour before the Workshop met to talk over critical attitudes. By the time we went into the classroom, we had a clear sequence of comments and the students benefitted greatly from having a variety of attitudes toward their work. It was like publishing then being re-

viewed. Don Justice and I differed enough in our approaches to poetry so that each supplied points of view which each might have omitted if teaching alone. In addition, whenever a student had enough poems or several stories, we saw him individually and it was in these conferences, so time-consuming, that much of the most effective criticism was achieved.[9]

In addition to his Workshop courses and conferences with individuals, Engle devoted considerable time to courses in the curriculum of the English Department proper. One of these, a course in contemporary literature, often attracted well over 200 students, and Engle read all the papers and exams himself.

The program's success was due in large part to Paul Engle's total commitment to it. Like John T. Frederick's commitment to the *Midland,* Engle viewed the Workshop as a personal cause and his own creation. His determination to run not only a first-rate program but the best in the country was evident in his continuous search for talent, his efforts in soliciting outside donations, and his work in securing publicity.

Not content to select his students from the applications that came unsolicited in the mail, Paul Engle—to use his own analogy—recruited writing talent the way a coach recruits athletic talent (although Engle paid his travel expenses himself). Over the years, he established a network of contacts with former students and such prominent teaching writers as Robert Penn Warren, Allen Tate, and John Crowe Ransom, who would send some of their best students to Iowa. Many people have attributed to Engle an uncanny ability to spot talent, sometimes on little evidence. Once convinced of a student's potential, Engle would go to great lengths to bring that student to Iowa City. The process was immensely time-consuming. His usual schedule of work included evenings in his "hog house" (a sobriquet for the shed he used as an office behind his house at Bayard Street), where he took care of his correspondence. Driven by a sense of urgency, he would personally deliver his letters to the Rock Island Railroad station every evening. As James B. Hall (a Workshop student in the late forties and early fifties) later explained:

> Paul seemed to live in a state of hypertension and each night at twelve o'clock he drove to the Iowa City railroad station to hand over his day's correspondence to the conductor so that the letters would be mailed the same night in Chicago. Engle typed all of his letters personally. They went out across the nation to new workshop candidates. Each term a new crop came to Iowa City and behind each arrival was a personal correspondence often of magnitude.[10]

Paul Engle in his backyard office, where he worked evenings conducting the correspondence of the Workshop's operation.

As a result of this personal attention, many students chose to attend Iowa even when they had been accepted by other prestigious programs that offered them a greater amount of financial aid.

One of Engle's more important distinctions as director was his remarkable success at fund raising. He undertook this task for the purpose of supplementing the financial awards made to his writers by the Graduate College. The chairman of the English Department, Baldwin Maxwell—whom Engle once described as "always considerate, always sympathetic toward an effort which must have seemed a curious one to him, and always a gentleman, even under pressure (and I must have been a real trial to him many times)"—would sit down with Engle, Maxwell with his pile of applications for scholarly students, Engle with his pile for writers. They would then alternate a scholar and a writer in their recommendations for Graduate College fellowships and scholarships. In spite of this just system of sharing available funds, Engle began soliciting contributions from outside sources to avoid what he has described as "the horror of being unable to bring here all of the talent" he had found.

Engle was aided in his search for funds by his reputation as a poet. First established when he won the Yale Series of Younger Poets Award, his reputation was advanced by a 1934 review of *American Song* on the front page of the *New York Times Book Review*. Later, the publication of his sixth collection of poetry, *American Child* (1945), a sonnet sequence, became the topic of an illustrated article in the September 23, 1946, issue of *Life* magazine. This prominence enabled him to present himself to the business world as a successful poet who not only was possessed of an unexpected measure of common sense and practicality but also was willing to sacrifice time from his own writing in order to raise money to help other writers. It was an unbeatable combination. While fund raising was often tremendously frustrating, Engle threw himself into the challenge with all the determination, enthusiasm, and forceful persuasiveness of which he was capable. By 1966, he estimated that he had raised personally some $375,000 in support of the program.[11] During his tenure as director of the International Writing Program, the total surpassed the two-million-dollar mark, a remarkable feat considering the relatively low tax-base provided by a predominantly agricultural state.

In addition to support from private businesses, grants from various foundations were essential to the growth of the Program in Creative Writing. The Workshop's role in administering the three-year $40,000 Rockefeller Foundation grant for writers brought the program considerable prestige. While the recipients were not required to enroll in the Workshop, in 1954 three of the five—Donald Justice, Jean Garrigue, and Verlin Cassill—were Iowa graduates. Over the years, the Workshop's most important sponsor was the Louis W. and Maud Hill Family Foundation (now the Northwest Area Foundation) of St. Paul, Minnesota, which awarded the Workshop a $45,000, three-year grant in 1962 and a $75,000, six-year grant in 1965. With the Foundation providing the backbone of outside support, the program mushroomed in size, peaking at over 250 graduate students in the academic year 1965–66.

Linked to Paul Engle's success at fund raising was his knack for obtaining publicity. An eloquent and convincing salesman armed with dramatic flair, Engle has for years provided fodder to journalists eager for the big story and the magic superlative. His instinct for the limelight, combined with an uncanny shrewdness, has produced remarkable results. In reference to an article in a national magazine that drew a flattering picture of the University and the Writers' Workshop, a friend of Engle's in publishing confided, "You are a marvelous obtainer of publicity, because the kind you obtain reads as if you had absolutely nothing to do with obtaining it." On the other hand, Engle takes exception to the assumption that securing publicity and raising funds came easily to him:

> Publicity and fund-raising are not peculiar gifts given some people and not others. Without proper and dignified publicity, with facts to back it up, no program can survive or even keep the reputation it once had. It took years of failure, years of finding the right approaches, to persuade newspapers and magazines to recognize the uniqueness and productivity of the Writers' Workshop. The same with money—it took years of failing, of refusing to accept NO as a suitable answer, before I learned about fund-raising. Self-taught, since no one in this University could give me practical advice (I speak of the humanities, since the sciences are a special case), I learned the hard and obstinate way, and not for self-aggrandizement, but for the Workshop.

Instead, his success at fund raising was the result of his determination and some "powerful" connections:

> I led a double life, doing my job in Iowa City, and visiting New York and Washington several times a year, not only because I had to go where the money was available, but also because, as a result of living in New York three years, I had many friends there and, if I may say so, powerful ones. These helped me get access to places where I would have had difficulty getting through the door (the Rockefellers, Harrimans, Mrs. Marshall Field, Mrs. John P. Marquand). I kept my mouth shut about this in Iowa City, but it was a very great help. Still, without hard evidence of the Workshop's excellence, none of this would have mattered. I was thrown out of some of the lushest offices in New York.

Unlike many faculty who go off to read and lecture for pay, I never left Iowa City without using the trip to solicit funds for the Workshop. [12]

Like his predecessors, Paul Engle recognized the value of well publicized conferences in drawing national attention to the University of Iowa program. The 1957 centennial of the publication of Charles Baudelaire's *Flowers of Evil* provided the occasion for the first of the big conferences engineered by Engle. Billed as "an act of homage which will help strengthen the cultural bonds between France and America," the event was celebrated on May 31 in Iowa City because, Engle maintained, the community's unusually high concentration of poets made it the "most appropriate" location in America for such a show of appreciation. Speakers included the eminent French scholar Marcel A. Ruff of the University of Aix-en-Provence, then visitor at the University of Chicago; Wallace Fowlie, author of several books on French poetry; Roger Shattuck of the University of Texas; W. R. Bandy of the University of Wisconsin; Donald Justice then of Hamline University; and Ralph Freedman of the University of Iowa faculty. The highlight of the centennial celebration was the publication by Harry Duncan's Cummington Press of *Homage to Baudelaire,* a book of poetry by sixteen Workshop poets. [13]

Not only did the event receive considerable coverage by the local press, but *Time* magazine ran an article entitled "Poets on the Farm" in its June 3 issue. The article's opening paragraph read:

> "We don't believe that we can make a poet out of a sow's ear," says Poet-Professor Paul Engle, "not even in Iowa, where we've got some damn fine sows' ears." But Paul Engle, 48, professor of English at the State University of Iowa in Iowa City, has fashioned the best workshop in the nation for young poets in an area surrounded by cows and corn.

After one paragraph describing the celebration and three paragraphs on Engle and the Workshop, the article concluded:

> In the Workshop, students gleefully lay into Engle's poems with the master's own tools of cutting criticism. But few critics carp at his ability as a teacher, and no one doubts his talents as a recruiter of potential poets. Even British Poet Stephen Spender has referred a prospect to him. [Paul] Englemen wrote fully one-third of the poems in *Poets Under Forty,* to be published this summer by the Meridian Press. And Henry Rago, editor of *Poetry* magazine, says: "No poet in the U.S. has done as much for young poets as Paul Engle." [14]

The following year, the University of Texas Press published a book entitled

The Centennial Celebration of Baudelaire's Les Fleurs du Mal, which was based on the papers read at the meeting.

The second big conference occurred on December 4 and 5, 1959, when the University of Iowa hosted the *Esquire* symposium. The general theme of the conference, "The Writer in a Mass Culture," was discussed by four prominent authors: Ralph Ellison, Mark Harris, Dwight MacDonald, and Norman Mailer. *Esquire's* editor-publisher Arnold Gingrich and Paul Engle served as moderators. It was estimated that more than 1,500 students, writers, critics, teachers, and professors from all over the country attended the symposium. Among them were literary editors of the *Des Moines Register, Chicago Daily News,* and *Chicago Sun-Times;* writing instructors from the University of Michigan, Carleton College, Grinnell College, and Principia College; and magazine editors and publishers of Meredith Publishing Company and Dial Press. In an article entitled "Eggheads in the Tall Corn," *Newsweek,* reporting that "something extraordinary and exciting was going on" in Iowa, seemed taken with the excitement and ambience generated by the conference. Later, in March of the following year, both *Esquire* and *Writer's Digest* magazines ran articles describing the "meeting of publisher and writer" in Iowa City. *Esquire* suggested that "Iowa and the students there had more effect on the writers than the writers had on them," and *Writer's Digest* quoted Gingrich as saying, "The academic centers are increasingly valuable breeding grounds for creative writing. And the most fertile of all the creative writing centers is Paul Engle's Writers' Workshop here in Iowa City."[15]

On May 3, 1960, only months after the *Esquire* symposium, Engle organized a luncheon for the friends of the Creative Writing Program. The event provided an occasion to announce two major projects. Bennett Cerf, the guest speaker and president of Random House, announced plans for publication of a volume of works by the writers involved in the program during the past twenty-five years. The second project was the founding of the Iowa Industries Fellowships in Writing, which were designed to bring young writers from all areas of the U.S. as well as other countries to Iowa.

The luncheon was repeated a year later as part of Creative Arts Week at the University of Iowa, which was held May 8–11, 1961. The week's festivities included a premiere performance of a new composition by noted French composer Darius Milhaud (commissioned by University of Iowa alumni), an Iowa art exhibit, performance of a song cycle by Philip Bezanson to texts by Paul Engle, other musical presentations, two dramatic productions, a lecture on poetry by W. D. Snodgrass (former Workshop poet and winner of the 1960 Pulitzer Prize in Poetry), readings of poetry written in the Workshop, and an on-the-spot demonstration of criticism of an original short story by the Fiction Workshop staff (which then included Vance Bourjaily, George Elliott, and Philip Roth).

But the most exciting news of the week was the appearance of the well publicized and much anticipated collection, *Midland: Twenty-Five Years of Fiction and Poetry Selected from the Writing Workshops of the State University of Iowa*, edited by Paul Engle, with assistance from Henri Coulette and Donald Justice. In addition to selections of some of the short stories and poems that were written by former students of the program, the collection contained an introduction in which Engle presented his argument in support of teaching creative writing in the academy and provided a list of distinctions achieved by Workshop writers. The collection drew national attention and was favorably reviewed in a number of important publications, including the *New York Herald-Tribune* and the *London Times Literary Supplement*. Five years later, plans were made to bring out a second selection to be entitled *Midland II*, but Random House was unwilling to take on the project because it had not "come out" on the first publication, in spite of heavy backing from Engle. Problems arose in making arrangements with another publisher and the project was finally abandoned.

Other accomplishments and activities by Engle that drew attention to the program included dozens of book reviews (written for such newspapers as the *Chicago Tribune*, the *New York Times*, and the *New York Herald-Tribune*); countless appearances and lectures; editorship from 1954–59 (with Hansford Martin, Constance Urdang, and Curt Harnack successively) of *Prize Stories: The O. Henry Awards*; a front page article entitled, "A Writer Is a Teacher Is a Writer," in the July 17, 1955, issue of the *New York Times Book Review* (in which Engle revealed that in those last three years students at Iowa had published seven novels, as well as numerous poems and short stories in respected magazines); co-editorship with Joseph Langland of a collection, entitled *Poet's Choice* (1956 and 1962), which included poems by "103 of the greatest living poets"; authorship of the libretto to Philip Bezanson's *Golden Child: A Christmas Opera* (telecast December 16, 1960, on the Hallmark Hall of Fame over NBC-TV); appointment in February 1962 to the program advisory committee of the proposed National Cultural Center (the Kennedy Center) in Washington, D.C. (Engle was the only member of the twelve-man committee who was not a resident of the New York–New Haven area); participation, along with W. D. Snodgrass, in the first National Poetry Festival held November 6, 1962, by the Library of Congress in Washington, D.C., in recognition of outstanding American poets (Engle let it be known that fourteen of the twenty-eight poets invited to read their works had appeared at some time on the University of Iowa campus); a four-month tour of Asia beginning in late January of 1963, funded by a $10,000 grant from the Rockefeller Foundation for the purpose of evaluating writing talent throughout the Asian countries (Engle's hope was "to find some talented young writers and ultimately to find ways of bringing them to the United States and especially to Iowa"); implementation of the first International Poetry Reading, held on the University campus on May 20, 1964 (the reading was taped by Voice of America for broadcast over its world-wide service, and special guests included: Donald Ranard, chief of the Far Eastern Office for the Bureau of Cultural and Educational Affairs for the Department of State; Porter McCray, director of the JDR 3rd Fund; Mrs. Bonnie Crown, director of the translation program at the Asia Society in New York; John Merriam, chairman of the board of Northern Natural Gas Company of Omaha; A. A. Heckman, executive director of the Louis W. and Maud Hill Family Foundation in Minnesota; and Charlotte Brooks, photographer for *Look*); production, in conjunction with the University of Iowa motion picture unit, of a twenty-four-minute, 16 mm. color film, entitled *Poetry: The World's Voice*, which was narrated by Engle and featured readings of nineteen poems in seventeen languages (the film was shown both locally and at the office of the Department of State in Washington, D.C., and at the offices of the United States Information Agency and the Voice of America in New York City); and appointment to a six-year term on the National Council on the Arts by President Johnson in February 1965 (Engle is the only poet to have served on the council).

The 1960s was the decade in which creative writing programs or "writers' workshops" became commonplace in universities and colleges across the country. Many of these programs were founded, directed, and staffed by Iowa Workshop graduates. (See "Appendix" for a list of names and programs.) Throughout this decade, University of Iowa Workshop writers continued to publish and gain recognition. A list of some (by no means all) of these successes follows.

In 1962, eleven of the thirty-five American poets in the second selection by Meridian Editions, *New Poets of England and America*, were associated with the Iowa Poetry Workshop. That same year Andrew Fetler won the *Atlantic Monthly* "First" award for his short story, "Longface." In 1964, *The Martyred*, a novel written by Richard Kim (a South Korean who had joined the Workshop in 1960), became a best seller. In February, Kim's novel was reviewed on the front page of the *New York Times Book Review* by Chad Walsh, who called it "a magnificent achievement" that "will last." Elsewhere, *The Martyred* received enthusiastic reviews, and articles on the novel appeared in *Life* and *Time* magazines.

In September of 1964, seven of the sixteen contributors to *Poetry* magazine were recent graduates of the University of Iowa Workshop, and in December of 1964, William Cotter Murray was named recipient of a $2,500 Meredith Press writing award for his first novel, *Michael Joe: A Novel of Irish Life*, which he began while a student in the Workshop. In 1965,

Henri Coulette's *The War of the Secret Agent and Other Poems* won the Lamont Poetry Selection, and in 1966 Margaret Walker Alexander received the Houghton Mifflin Literary Fellowship for her novel, *Jubilee,* which she had submitted as her Ph.D. thesis in the Workshop.[16] In 1967, James Tate was awarded the Yale Series of Younger Poets Award for his collection, *The Lost Pilot,* and Clark Blaise won the President's Medal of the Canadian Authors Association for the best short story published in Canada.

During the early and mid-sixties, which was the last part of Engle's term as director, the faculty consisted at various times of George P. Elliott, Eugene Garber, Philip Roth, Edmund Keeley, David Pryce-Jones, Mark Strand, Richard Yates, William Cotter Murray, George Starbuck, Marvin Bell, Nelson Algren, Kurt Vonnegut, José Donoso, Paul Carroll, Robert Sward, Donald Justice, Vance Bourjaily, and R. V. Cassill.

NOTES

1   Wallace Stegner, "New Climates for the Writer," *The Writer in America* (Osaka: Hokuseido Press, 1951), pp. 52–54.

2   The poets included were Ricaredo Demetillo, Albert Herzing, Cynthia Pickard, Arthur Covell, William Stafford, Edith Tiempo, Peter Hald (a pseudonym for Donald Petersen), Dominador I. Ilio, David Clay Jenkins, William Belvin, James B. Hall, J. V. Meade, Courtney Johnson, and Robert Shelley.

3   Flannery O'Connor published "The Geranium" in *Accent* (Summer 1946) and "The Train" in *Sewanee Review* (Spring 1948). In an article entitled "Flannery O'Connor: A Reminiscence and Some Letters," which appeared in *North American Review,* 255 (Spring 1970), 58–60, Jean Wylder wrote of O'Connor's stay in Iowa City:

> My first impression of Flannery O'Connor was that she looked too young and too shy to be a writer. . . . On the opening day of class, Flannery was sitting alone in the front row, over against the wall. She was wearing what I was soon to think of as her "uniform" for that year: plain gray skirt and neatly-ironed silkish blouse, nylon stockings and penny brown loafers. Her only makeup was a trace of lipstick. Elizabeth Hardwick once described her as "like some quiet, puritanical convent girl from the harsh provinces of Canada"; there *was* something of the convent about Flannery that day—a certain intentness in the slight girlish figure which set her apart from the rest of us. She seemed out of place in that room composed mostly of veterans returned from World War II. Flannery was only 22 years old then, but she could easily have passed for 17 or 18. . . .
>
> It was her isolation from the other "Writers" in the class that first drew me to her, and soon that semester I moved to the empty seat beside her. We and one

other girl were the only women in the Workshop that year. Most of the others, the former GI's, were tuned-in to New Criticism theories, and many sensitive young writers got shot down by the heavy onslaught of their critical fire. Stories were dissected like so many literary specimens; few stood up under the minute probing. . . .

Her favorite place to go in Iowa City was out to the City Park. Once, I walked out there with her on an especially bleak February Sunday afternoon to look at the two sad and mangy bears, the raccoons, and the special foreign chickens they had. It seemed a particularly desultory thing to be doing, and I was puzzled at how completely absorbed and interested Flannery was that day looking at these things which I knew she'd looked at many times before. She was still working on the novel then, of course (which was to be *Wise Blood*), although she never talked about it, and I knew nothing at that time about the zoo and park scenes in that book until I read it a few years later. But, I also realize now, her fondness for the zoo went beyond the fact that she may have been getting "material" for her work.

Later in a letter which Wylder quotes, O'Connor commented on housing in Iowa City and recalled the park:

I remember those boarding houses in Iowa City very well and all the cold rooms I looked at. My landlady, Mrs. Guzeman [at 115 E. Bloomington Street], was not very fond of me because I stayed at home and required heat to be on—at least ON. It was never UP that I remember. When it was on you could smell it and I got to where I warmed up a little every time I smelled it. One of these days I would like to see Iowa City again, but only for the zoo where those game bantams were and the bears donated by the Iowa City Lions Club.

4   The interview from which this excerpt is taken appeared in the *North American Review*, 262 (Summer 1977), 7–15, which also featured interviews with Donald Justice and Marvin Bell.

5   Information based on Jay Walljasper, *"Defender,* dawn of underground press," *Daily Iowan*, November 29, 1976.

6   1949 *University of Iowa Catalogue*, p. 65.

7   1957 *University of Iowa Catalogue*, p. 76.

8   The Translation Workshop was organized with the help of John Gerber and Ralph Freedman and subsequently taught by Mark Strand, Frederick Will, and David Hayman.

9   Quoted from Paul Engle's written response to the first draft of the chapter on the "Engle Workshop," University of Iowa Archives, Iowa City.

10   James B. Hall to Jean Wylder, "Writers' Workshop: Reminiscences," in University of Iowa Archives, Iowa City.

11   Roy Reynolds, "Poet Engle's Fund-Raising at Iowa University Called Unique," *Des Moines Register* (February 15, 1966), p. 6. The most regular contributors to the program included Sutherland Dows and Iowa Electric Light and Power of Cedar Rapids, J. W. Fisher and Fisher Governor Co. of Marshalltown, Mrs. Fred Maytag of Newton, Gardner Cowles and the Cowles Charitable Trust of Des Moines and New York, William B. Quarton and WMT of Cedar Rapids, Howard Hall and Iowa Manufacturing Co. of Cedar Rapids, and Northern Natural Gas of Omaha.

12 Quoted from Paul Engle's written response to the first draft of the chapter on the "Engle Workshop," University of Iowa Archives, Iowa City.

13 *Homage to Baudelaire* was edited by Paul Engle and included work by the following poets: Peter Everwine, Theodore Holmes, Raeburn Miller, Donald Justice, Philip Levine, John Taylor, Paulene Aspel, Richard McDougall (as translator), Harry Duncan (as translator), Paul Engle, Henri Coulette, Paul Petrie, Robert Mezey, and Alfredo A. Roggiano.

14 "Poets on the Farm," *Time* (June 3, 1957), 39.

15 "Eggheads in the Tall Corn," *Newsweek* (December 28, 1959), 65–66; "Athens in the Cornfields," *Esquire*, 53 (1960), 6; *Writer's Digest*, 40 (1960).

16 Aside from the publicity derived from publication by Workshop students and faculty, the Workshop's reputation was also given a boost by the following articles: "The State University of Iowa," *Time* (September 6, 1954), in which the Workshop receives a favorable mention; "Classes with a poet," *Mademoiselle* (November 1954), in which Mary Jane Baker describes her experience in a poetry class with Robert Lowell; "A Town of Many Talents," *Saturday Review* (July 1961), one of many articles in response to the publication of *Midland*, in which Rust Hills describes Iowa City as "the only non-Bohemian literary community in America" and lauds Engle for his pioneering work; "The Muses Meet in Squaresville," *Mademoiselle* (November 1961), in which David Boroff offers one of the most perceptive portrayals of the Workshop that has appeared; "Iowa, A Very Far Country Indeed," *Esquire* (December 1962), in which Philip Roth, as an easterner in a small midwestern town, takes a critical view of Iowa City (an article considered by some to have damaged indirectly the Workshop's reputation); "Creative Education," *Writer's Digest* (1962), in which Kirk Polking offers one of the most detailed portrayals that has appeared; "The Structure of the American Literary Establishment," *Esquire* (July 1963), in which Rust Hills referred to the Workshop as "the most important" program on a college campus—forty-two former SUI students or faculty members (or one-third of the total) are included in the listing of what the magazine terms "everyone of any serious literary consequence"; "State University of Iowa," *Holiday* (November 1963), in which Calvin Kentfield provides a candid portrait of campus goings-on (which some University officials found offensive) and offers praise to the Workshop; and "University of Iowa's Paul Engle, Poet-Grower to the World," *Look* (June 1, 1965), in which T. George Harris gives a flattering view of how the Workshop works. More recent articles include Clarence Petersen's article (which appeared in the April 28, 1968, issue of *Chicago Sun-Times Magazine*), and Gail Godwin's sensitively written "The Iowa Experience" (which appeared in the January 10, 1975, issue of *New Times*). Nelson Algren's "At play in the fields of hack-ademe" (which appeared in the October 21, 1973, issue of the *Chicago Tribune Magazine)* is a spirited, full-fledged attack and denunciation of the Workshop's concept of teaching creative writing in a university environment. (See "Bibliography" for complete citations.)

Controversy

DURING THE GROWTH of the Workshop and the establishment of its reputation, the administration of the program was not without its conflicts. Prior to the upheaval of 1964–66, during which Paul Engle resigned his directorship and two ranking faculty members resigned angrily from the University, an incident occurred which pitted Engle against every other full-time professor of the English Department and exacerbated long-standing tensions between some of the department's "writers" and "scholars."

When Ray B. West, Jr., returned to Iowa in 1949 as an associate professor in the Creative Writing Program (he first came to Iowa in the summer of 1940 on a teaching assistantship), he brought with him the *Western Review* (founded in Utah in 1936 as the *Rocky Mountain Review*). West came with the understanding that his literary magazine would be subsidized enough to allow payment to contributors, and he was given three credit hours of "released time" to edit the magazine.

In 1957, while Ray West was in Turkey on a Rockefeller Foundation Fellowship, Paul Engle (who was then out of town) sent a letter to Dean Loehwing recommending that publication of the *Western Review* be suspended at once and that the funds which had gone to its support be diverted to fellowships for graduate students in creative writing. When Baldwin Maxwell received a copy of Engle's letter on Friday, May 24, he at once called upon the dean to express his non-concurrence in Professor Engle's recommendation. He indicated that he felt strongly that a sudden withdrawal of all support at a time when he [West] was abroad and entertained no suspicion of such action, would appear grossly unfair and would seriously damage the morale and well-being of the department. At issue here was the degree of the Workshop's independence from the rest of the English Department. In spite of Maxwell's efforts, Loehwing decided in favor of suspension and posted a letter informing West of the decision.

On June 3, Maxwell sent a letter to Dean Loehwing tracing the chronology of events in the matter and protesting the precipitate decision. To assure the dean that Maxwell had not misrepresented the views of the department, every full-time professor except two had appended his or her signature to the letter. (The two exceptions were then out of the city but both of them, Maxwell was certain, would have wished to sign.) On June 4, Maxwell sent a copy of the letter to Engle along with a cover letter in which he asked Engle to request the dean to withdraw the actions he had taken and to postpone a final decision until Ray's comment could be received.

Engle refused. He argued that the Graduate College had repeatedly expressed concern over the magazine's small number of subscribers in proportion to the cost of subsidizing the publication and that the magazine had been giving increasing emphasis to criticism over creative work, while the latter was the only interest of the Creative Writing Program. With the funds previously committed to the *Western Review,* Engle wanted to finance a new fellowship program for writers. He pointed out that if action were not taken then but at the end of the next year, it would mean a three-year delay in implementing such a program. In a letter to University President Virgil Hancher, he explained the urgent need of the fellowships and expressed his willingness to resign over the issue:

> This year, we lost *all* of the top students who applied: the finest writer at Wellesley was offered $250.00, and accepted $2,500.00 from Stanford, although I had put her at the top of my list of recommendations. A man who graduated *summa* from Harvard was given nothing. Three others are going to Stanford, Wisconsin, Michigan. . . .
>
> In brief, the coming year will be a mediocre year, save for a handful of carry-overs from this year, and older students wanting to return. All I requested was the substitution of two or three graduate fellowships, to the best writers in this country, for the *Western Review.* This is the minimum capable of keeping SUI at the only place which matters—the top.
>
> Because of my recommendation, I was presented with a reproach by my colleagues, with open insults, with accusations that my only concern was to advance my private profit, and with charges of injustice to Ray West, who had left the USA after filing a report, requested nine months before, the day before he left.
>
> I can, of course, not consider continuing as "director" (an honorary and chance title) of the writing program, when each time that I try to act in a way which seems not only best for the writing program but for the University as a whole, I am forced to defend myself against the more aggressive of my colleagues, who are always the least productive members of the department.[1]

In response to the intensity of the faculty's feeling, the decision to suspend the *Western Review* was reversed until Ray West's side of the case could be presented. In a twenty-page report defending the journal and itemizing past expenses, West referred to the University's honorable record in its support of such literary magazines. He also quoted highly favorable comments on his publication by Lionel Trilling, Allen Tate, Robert Penn Warren, Walter Van Tilburg Clark, and Robert Lowell. West concluded his argument by observing that a good many graduate students, who had been attracted to the State University of Iowa, had stated that they had come primarily because they knew that the Writers' Workshop at the State University of Iowa sponsored one of the best literary magazines in the country. Although it was decided ultimately to continue subsidizing the *Western Review*, in 1959 Ray West had an opportunity to merge his magazine with *Contact* in San Francisco. At that time he submitted his resignation.

The incident involving Engle and West was preceded by a history of strained relations between the two men. Earlier, West had vigorously opposed Engle's decision to terminate Hansford (Mike) Martin's appointment as a Workshop instructor. (Martin had been appointed lecturer in 1947 and assistant professor in 1949. He resigned in June 1955.) The dispute drew fire from certain English Department faculty members who felt that Engle's decision was based on his disapproval of Martin's lifestyle rather than an honest assessment of Martin's competence. Engle maintained that he had "carried Martin along" for some time, despite Martin's not having published since his arrival in Iowa City. He also pointed to the fact that Martin was a personal friend who had often been a guest at his home. A Workshop instructor backed Engle by asserting that Martin himself was aware of his diminishing effectiveness, which was caused by his drinking, and that he had equivocated about continuing in his post. Of equal importance to the question of Engle's motives was the feeling among the Workshop faculty that certain Engle-detractors in the English Department proper were using the incident to launch what Verlin Cassill later described as a "campaign of calumny" which was "orchestrated through the cocktail party circuit . . . with the obvious aim of discrediting Paul."[2] At the time of Engle's efforts to suspend the *Western Review*, hard feelings persisted on both sides.

The upheaval of 1964–66 is explained best in this context. Beginning in the fall of 1964, plans were being made for the next year's administration of the Workshop while Engle was abroad. At the time, Engle, tiring of the directorship and eager to devote more time to his writing, was considering the possibility of playing a less active role in the Workshop's administration upon his return. Also, because of the program's increasing enrollment, it was generally agreed that the Workshop's director needed an assistant to free him of some of his administrative duties. Various plans were discussed, one involving Richard Lloyd-Jones serving as a kind of program manager with Donald Justice taking care of the Poetry Workshop and Robert Williams in charge of the Fiction Workshop; another with Donald Justice as acting head of the entire program; and yet another with Donald Justice and Robert Williams as co-directors. It was generally understood that Verlin Cassill, a novelist with seniority over Robert Williams, was not interested in administrative duties. Part of the problem in deciding on a plan was apprehension on the part of Engle's nominated successors. As Donald Justice (who was then in San Francisco on a Ford Foundation Fellowship) made clear in a letter, no member of the present writing staff was qualified to take on the whole responsibility Paul Engle had borne, chiefly in the matter of fund-raising from outside sources. Paul Engle and John Gerber (who had succeeded Baldwin Maxwell as English Department chairman) were conferring on the matter, though no details of their consultations were recorded in writing.

On January 27, 1965, John Gerber made an offer to Robert Williams of an appointment as associate professor. Prior to this, Engle had left town for showings of his new film, *Poetry: The World's Voice*, in Washington and New York. Shortly thereafter, Gerber, who was then serving as head of Project English in the U.S. Office of Education, left for Chicago. When Verlin Cassill heard the news of the offer to Williams, he was shocked and infuriated. He called together a number of Workshop staff members and students at his home, where he charged that there was a conspiracy afoot to downgrade the Workshop's status in relation to the English Department by altering the balance of power among the Workshop faculty. Cassill also interpreted the move as an attempt to downgrade his own standing by promoting a relative newcomer over him. W. R. Irwin, director of graduate studies, called Gerber in Chicago to inform him, "All hell has broken loose." Engle, upon his return to Iowa City on February 1, denied any knowledge of a decision to extend the offer. Although bitter feelings between Engle and Gerber developed as a result of the dispute, the real heat of the controversy was generated by the clash between Gerber and Cassill. Cassill was convinced (as Engle was not) that Gerber was scheming to "annex" the Workshop, to bring it more directly under his control.

As was true of the earlier episodes, the dispute was called "The Battle between the Hut and the Hill," in reference to the Workshop's location in the barracks down by the river and the English Department's location in the more imposing buildings up on the Pentacrest. And as in the past, the conflict created factions among faculty members and strained relations between the Workshop and the English Department. But this time the dispute seemed more serious in nature: rumors began to spread around the country that the University of Iowa Workshop's effectiveness as an educational institution was in jeopardy.[3]

On the evening of February 5, a meeting involving Gerber, Irwin, Engle, Cassill, and Vance Bourjaily took place at Engle's home. Engle had returned from New York with a case of influenza so severe that he lay on the sofa as they talked and the day after the meeting he was hospitalized. Gerber had requested the conference in hopes of resolving the dispute, but later admitted that "it got us nowhere." At that meeting he emphasized to Cassill that, the day before the offer was made to Williams, he had also recommended a raise in Cassill's salary which would have given him an amount considerably larger than that offered to Williams. Gerber also tried to convince Cassill that making the actual offer to Williams in advance of a firm decision on Cassill's case was a routine procedural matter necessitated by the fact that Williams was then in the position of having to accept or decline an offer elsewhere. Unsatisfied by the explanation, Cassill requested that he too be considered for an associate professorship. He went on to state that, unless Gerber found the means to re-establish the balance of power that had been upset, he would have no choice but to resign his post.

On February 10, Engle wrote to Gerber from Mercy Hospital in Iowa City. In this letter, Engle maintained his claim that he had not been consulted about the promotion of Williams and spoke of the loyalty he felt toward his staff. Engle also pointed out the department's obligation to recognize his own exceptional service to the University by offering him a fair salary and provided a list of points that he considered essential to the well-being of the program. The most urgent of these was his recommendation that Bourjaily and Cassill be promoted to the rank of associate professor (Justice was already an associate professor) and that all three men should be given salaries "substantially" higher than the $11,000 offered to Williams.

On the same day that Engle wrote to Gerber from Mercy Hospital, there was a meeting of the full professors, who recommended that Vance Bourjaily be promoted to the rank of associate professor. Engle was neither notified of the meeting nor consulted by phone. When he found out, he referred to the action as "the second such appointment to be made without consultation with the so-called 'Director' of the Program." He protested on these grounds:

> I submit that for the Full Professors to presume to make tenure appointments to the Program in Creative Writing without first securing the opinion of the Director (who has always consulted his staff in every such matter) was contrary to all previous practise, and an exer-

cise of authority in an arrogant manner. For the Professors to pass over Cassill, without even inquiring whether he wished such appointment, and without asking the Director his views, was a further error.

In the same letter, Engle also revealed his knowledge of another matter. He had discovered that there had been a meeting between Gerber and Bourjaily during his January absence and that questions of rank, tenure, and salary in regard to Williams had been discussed. His comment on the previously undisclosed meeting was:

> I do not consider this is in any way improper, but courtesy and tact should have meant that Engle was to be informed of the discussion, especially prior to any offer to Williams. Engle should certainly have been informed of this when the whole question of how Williams was appointed arose.[4]

Meanwhile, Verlin Cassill had submitted his resignation. The committee on appointments and promotions—Engle included—refused to accept the resignation and voted to ask Cassill to withdraw it and to meet with his classes for the remainder of the semester. In an informal discussion with Cassill and Engle on the evening of February 15, Gerber advised Cassill not to push for any decision on tenure or promotion for at least a month. Gerber promised that if there could be such a cooling-off period, he would call a special meeting of the committee to consider Cassill's claims for tenure and promotion.

Cassill agreed to withdraw his resignation. However, according to Gerber, no such cooling-off period ensued. "Almost immediately thereafter," Gerber wrote in a memorandum placed in Cassill's file, "he and his friends began a steady attack, orally and in letters, on certain individuals and groups within the Department. The Department of English will review Mr. Cassill's claims to tenure but not while subject to duress which is both unjustified and unjustifiable."[5] Petitions stating that Cassill was indispensable to the Workshop were circulated around the campus and town. One Workshop student (André Dubus) wrote a letter praising Cassill as a dedicated teacher and lamenting the institution's blow to the cause of honor and goodness.[6] A copy of the letter was sent to Gerber, another was sent to University President Howard Bowen, and another was displayed for all to see on the Workshop's bulletin board. Finally, a group of Cassill's students (led by André Dubus, John Fontenot, and Jim Whitehead) planned to organize a march on the Pentacrest but were dissuaded from their intentions by Engle, who argued that such a public protest might do more harm than good.

Verlin Cassill, for his part, later recalled that for a period lasting from mid-winter to the following summer, after he had been persuaded to withdraw his letter of resignation, he was "left dangling, with no voice in whatever administrative discussions were going on and no certainty about my future." He was convinced that he "had been disarmed by the ploy" over his letter of resignation. Furthermore, Cassill maintained that at no time did he ask for a penny's increase in salary. His reason for requesting tenure was that tenure would ensure him of the right to express his views without fear of reprisal. When asked later if his initial response to the news of Williams's promotion was caused by an undisclosed desire to become Engle's successor, Cassill answered that it was not. While he did recall making "a tactical offer to assume the directorship" during the spring of 1965, he asserted, "I had no real notion that such a proposal would be acceptable to any of the contending powers—or I probably would not have made it."[7] During the academic year 1965–66, R. V. Cassill served as writer-in-residence at Purdue University. He returned to Iowa in the summer of 1966, but changed his mind about staying and accepted an offer from Brown University.

Donald Justice, one of the four ranking members of the Workshop faculty, was on leave during the upheaval in the winter and spring of 1964–65. Although he was in town briefly in February for the purpose of helping with negotiations, he spent the remainder of the semester in Florida. Because of previous inequities between his salary and that of other Workshop instructors, and due to the intensity of the outburst over the Williams promotion, Justice had serious misgivings about returning to Iowa in the fall. He was finally persuaded by Engle to give it a try, but he remained doubtful of the future in view of the pervasive bitterness created by the continuing dispute. When Justice returned to Iowa City and dis-covered that Paul Engle's proposal to increase his salary from funds in the Workshop's budget had been rejected, but that funds had been committed to a new salary line for support staff, he promptly submitted his resigna-tion (to go into effect at the close of that academic year).

As for Robert Williams, his role might be described best as that of an innocent culprit. In the initial negotiations concerning his salary, he had used the standing offer of a job at California State University at Hayward as a bargaining chip for inducing Gerber to offer him more money to stay at Iowa. When Williams informed the University of California of the in-creased offer from Iowa, California matched that amount in *its* offer, and when Williams then informed Gerber of the increased offer from Cal-ifornia, Gerber again raised *his* offer. So Williams came out the winner, but in winning failed to recognize the deadly seriousness with which his colleagues were playing the game. No doubt bewildered by the sudden fury and continuing intensity of the melee that ensued, Williams had second thoughts about staying and returned to California in the fall of 1965.

Perhaps the person most capable of assessing John Gerber's motives in the affair is Eugene Garber, whom both Engle and Cassill describe as a "man of perfect integrity." Garber, who stepped in as an unofficial but very capable director in the fall of 1965, has written:

> During the year and a half or so I was pinch-hitting for Paul or was co-ordinating things in the absence of any director at all, I of course worked closely with the chairman, John Gerber, and with several departmental committees. Gerber was very co-operative and supportive during this time. The allotment of TA's and scholarships to the workshop was very generous. I mention this because I think at one time some few have tried to suggest that Gerber wanted to co-opt or perhaps even smother the workshop. Nothing in my experience suggests that that was true. . . . And there were many other friends of the workshop in the department: Bob Scholes, Ralph Freedman, Sven Armens, Carl Klaus, Jix Lloyd-Jones, Bob Irwin. It would be easy, I think, to play up the creative vs academic stuff. That tension was there, sure, but the big blow-ups were more personality than ideology, I think.[8]

In retrospect, it would seem that the cause of the dispute was administrative misunderstanding on the part of both Paul Engle and John Gerber. When the initial misunderstanding occurred, both men were preoccupied with other projects and activities: Engle was in New York for showings of his film on the Program in Creative Writing and Gerber was in Chicago for a meeting relating to his position as head of Project English. Given these circumstances—compounded by the fact that the program's rapidly increasing enrollment was complicating the operation of the Workshop—it is not surprising that a breakdown in communication occurred. Whether or not a firm agreement on Williams's appointment had in fact been reached by Engle and Gerber (Engle maintains that had he made such a recommendation he would have done so in writing as was his practice, and Gerber has declared, "I will swear to my dying day that Engle met with me and indicated that he wanted Robert Williams to be offered an associate professorship"), more direct consultations among everyone involved might have allayed the suspicion and outright distrust that prevailed. As director of the Writers' Workshop and as head of the English Department, it was Engle's and Gerber's joint responsibility to see that no one was taken by surprise in regard to changes in the Workshop's administrative structure.

1 Engle to Virgil Hancher, June 12, 1957, copy in Engle's personal papers.

2 Verlin Cassill, letter to the author, August 26, 1976, "Workshop Correspondence with Wilbers," no. 226, University of Iowa Archives, Iowa City.

3 Margaret Walker Alexander, who was a student during this period, has described in *How I Wrote Jubilee* (Chicago: Third World Press, 1972, pp. 22–23) the controversy's impact on her personally:

> I had always had the fear that before I could finish the book Verlin Cassill would be out of the Writers' Workshop, and that winter he suddenly began to threaten to leave. Some six weeks passed before a dispute in the Workshop had cooled down enough for Cassill to look at my manuscript. Meanwhile I was sick with apprehension and fear over the possible departure of my key faculty reader. But just as I thought it would drive me to physical illness, Miss Hovey decided that she would read each page I wrote. Then we discussed it in terms of the whole story and she commented and made suggestions, either approving or disagreeing. That saved the day. By February 22, 1965, I had completed the second section, that terrible Civil War—which my husband declared he had been fighting all the twenty-odd years of our marriage. I celebrated by going to the movies and going out with friends to dinner.

4 Engle, "A Chronology," included in a letter to Gerber, March 2, 1965, copy in Engle's personal papers and in Department of English Records.

5 Verlin Cassill's file was examined by the author only after written permission was received from both Mr. Gerber and Mr. Cassill. Information and wording in this paragraph and above were based on this memorandum.

6 Andre Dubus's letter read in part: "If the petty and small and gray side of man wins at the Writers' Workshop, then one must conclude that it has won everywhere. One has to stop believing in places, in institutions; then one has to turn to himself, and that's rather lonely."

7 When he left Iowa for good in the fall of 1966, Verlin Cassill ended a long and passionate (if notorious) affiliation with the University of Iowa. A midwesterner by origin, he had been a member of Engle's first class when Engle returned to Iowa in 1937. Cassill received his bachelor of arts degree from Iowa in 1939, his master's degree in 1947, and from 1948 to 1952 served as an instructor and assistant professor. After living for a time in Paris and in New York City, he returned to Iowa in 1960.

A man possessed of a deep sense of regional pride, R. V. Cassill was convinced that he was fighting a battle in defense of the unique awareness and atmosphere that he recognized as indigenous to Iowa City. As he saw it, it was the same battle fought by Edwin Ford Piper and John T. Frederick during the nineteen-tens, twenties, and thirties, a struggle to assert and defend a particular attitude or perspective toward one's surroundings. Although the issue of regional awareness was largely forgotten amidst the new spirit of the war and postwar years, for Cassill it was very much alive in the 1960s and he viewed his conflict with John Gerber in this light. In a letter to the author (no. 226), Cassill wrote:

I was not uninformed about the way such things were done in Iowa City. I recalled the Nailing of Norman Foerster. (I had in fact tried to cite it during the hassle of the previous spring, intending to bring it up as an example of dishonorable academic politics that should not be repeated by the Nailing of Paul Engle.) I recalled the assassination of Grant Wood's artistic reputation by successors who meant thereby to aggrandize their own. I considered the ongoing persistence of the campaign of slurs, rumor and innuendo to which Paul had been subjected for a very long time, a partly subterranean campaign, orchestrated through the cocktail-party circuit by members of other departments as well as the English staff. . . .

For all the cosmopolitan complexion given by teachers and students from everywhere, the Workshop came to a head as an expression—and indeed as an asylum—for a kind of awareness of the modern scene and modern letters crisply different from that found in, say, New York, San Francisco, London, Paris. One's intuitions, one's "better mind" acknowledged this distinct flavor, and people who were any good respected it. The enemies of light could always be identified by their disparagement of what they found it advantageous to scoff at as "regionalism." At its continuing best, the awareness begat in Iowa City was perfectly capable of discriminating between provincialism and its own unique spirit. Of discriminating between fame and celebrity. Between the power of potency and the power of coercion. It appreciated the risk of flaunting such distinctions under the noses of coercive powers.

8 Eugene Garber, in a letter to the author, July 6, 1976, no. 202, "Workshop Correspondence with Wilbers," University of Iowa Archives, Iowa City.

Postscript
1966–80

BEYOND the loss of Cassill, the temporary loss of Justice (who rejoined the faculty in 1971), and the loss of Engle to the program (but not to the University), the upheaval's effects on the Workshop included a general decline in morale and a pervasive feeling that the program was without direction. Longer lasting effects involved changes in the administrative and financial structures of the Workshop. A full-time administrative assistant was added to the program in 1971. As for funding, outside donations to the Workshop (which in Engle's last years were averaging $40,000-$50,000) have all but disappeared, with the notable exception of a gift from the James A. Michener Fund in 1980. (This $500,000 fund, made available through the generosity of Mr. Michener, and administered by the Copernicus Society of America, will provide a series of annual grants to young American prose writers intended to aid them in publication of their work.) The program now depends on its regular allotment from the English Department and the Graduate College. This shift from external to internal funding has brought a steadier and more secure income.

The basic relationship between the Writers' Workshop and the rest of the Department of English has not changed appreciably. As before, the Workshop is a program within the Department of English, which means the faculty of the English Department continues to pass on promotions in the Workshop. The Workshop faculty, outside the core of tenured faculty, is made up of visiting instructors whose stay is limited (by precedent) to a period of two years. Although these appointments must be approved officially by the chairman of the Department of English, in practice they are handled by the permanent faculty of the Workshop.

In spite of periods of conflict between individuals on the Workshop staff and some members of the department, during most of the Workshop's history cordiality has prevailed. Most members of the English Department have been happy to have young writers in their classes. They realize that the Workshop has been responsible for bringing some of their best students to Iowa. To be sure, a minority has disapproved of the whole idea of combining imaginative writing with traditional graduate study in preparation for a Ph.D., but the department as a whole has supported and continues to support the Workshop as an activity and as an institution.

Ironically, the crisis of 1964–66 provided Paul Engle with an opportunity of bringing to bear his considerable experience, influence, and determination in organizing a new program. By freeing him from a twenty-eight-year preoccupation with the Writers' Workshop, the dispute enabled Engle to plan the International Writing Program.

When he left Iowa in the fall of 1965 for nine months of studying and writing in Europe, Engle had resigned as Workshop director and arrangements had been made for a "promotion" upon his return. The purpose of the specially created professorship, known as the Clarke Fisher Ansley Professor of Creative Writing, was to free Engle of specific administrative duties in the Workshop while allowing him to maintain a relationship with the program as an adviser, teacher, and poet. But no sooner was he freed of these duties than he began formulating a plan for administering a new program.

The program, originally to be called the Center of International Writing, was conceived as an extension of the Program in Creative Writing. At this stage, it was more a development of an earlier idea than an innovation. Since the 1950s, Engle had been bringing to Iowa City writers from Ireland, Japan, Taiwan, South Korea, the Philippines, Iran, Canada, England, and Sweden, and by the time the Translation Workshop was established in 1963 Engle was already considering the possibility of making Iowa City a unique international center.

The suggestion to develop the center, along with the translation workshop, into a separate program came from Hualing Nieh, the well known Chinese novelist and translator who in 1964 had come to Iowa City as consultant to the Translation Workshop. When the new program was established as the International Writing Program, she became its associate director.

The purpose of the International Writing Program is to bring prominent foreign writers to Iowa City, provide them with free time for their writing, and give them a leisurely view of American life. While here, the visiting writers work in collaboration with American writers on first editions of their work in English. This method of co-translation is designed to produce an English version that is not only syntactically and idiomatically accurate, but that has—in Engle's words—"a tone that does not reek of the translator's sweat."

Since the establishment of the International Writing Program (announced formally on June 9, 1967), six books of translations have been published by the University of Iowa Press as part of its Iowa Translations Series. One of the more recent publications of the International Writing

Program, entitled *Writing from the World* (1976), is an anthology representing twenty-seven languages and featuring the work of sixty-nine one-time participants in the program. In recognition of their efforts to promote communication between articulate peoples of the world, Paul Engle and Hualing Nieh (who were married in 1971) were nominated in February 1976 by present and former participants in the program for the Nobel Peace Prize.

In the years since Paul Engle's tenure as director of the Writers' Workshop, the program's reputation has been upheld by the continuing prominence of its faculty and graduates. The faculty of the Workshop under George Starbuck included Ted Berrigan, Anselm Hollo, Richard Yates, Jon Silkin, William Price Fox, Robert Coover, Courtland (C. D. B.) Bryan, Robert Boles, Mary Carter, Jack Marshall, Kathleen Fraser, Steven Katz, David Ray, Michael Dennis Browne, and Gina Berriault.

Under John Leggett, who was appointed acting director in 1970 and the Workshop's fourth director in 1971, the faculty has consisted of Galway Kinnell, Richard Hugo, Seymour Krim, Bienvenido Santos, Barry Goldensohn, Dan Wakefield, Angus Wilson, Ann Birstein, Helen Chasin, Fred Exley, Gail Godwin, John Irving, Stephen Becker, Ray Carver, John Cheever, Norman Dubie, Stanley Elkin, William Price Fox, Mark Strand, Henry Bromell, Jane Howard, Sandra McPherson, Stanley Plumly, Charles Wright, Carolyn Kizer, Leonard Michaels, Thomas Rogers, Mary Lee Settle, Jon Anderson, Robert Anderson, Fred Busch, Rosalyn Drexler, Louise Gluck, Frank Conroy, Bill Matthews, Richard Murphy, Arturo Vivante, Elizabeth Cullinan, Ian McEwan, Edward Hoagland, Hilma Wolitzer, Stephen Dobyns, Judith Moffett, Henry Carlile, David Hughes, Nicholas Delbranco, Bharati Mukherjee, Robert Kirsch, Janet Burroway, and Doris Grumbach.

A partial list of some of the major awards won in recent years by Workshop graduates follows. In 1968, Jane Cooper (1954 M.A.) won the Lamont Poetry Selection and Robert Bly (1956 M.A.) won the National Book Award. The following year, Marvin Bell (1963 M.F.A.) won the Lamont Poetry Selection and Charles Wright (1963 M.F.A.) won the Eunice Tietjens Award. In 1971, Stephen Dobyns (1967 M.F.A.) won the Lamont Poetry Selection and Peter Klappert (1968 M.F.A.) received the Yale Series of Younger Poets Award. Philip Levine (1957 M.F.A.) won the Frank O'Hara Memorial Prize and Pete Everwine (1959 Ph.D.) won the Lamont in 1972. The following year, Steve Orlen (1967 M.F.A.) was awarded the George Dillon Memorial Award and Theodore Weesner (1968 M.F.A.) won a Martha Foley Best Short Stories Award. In 1974, Donald Finkel (who attended the Workshop in 1955–56 and in the fall of 1957) won the Theodore Roethke Memorial Award, Mark Strand (1962 M.A.) won the

John Leggett was appointed the Workshop's fourth director in 1971.

Edgar Allan Poe Award, and Michael Ryan (1974 Ph.D.) won the Yale Series. In 1975, Thomas Williams (who studied in the Workshop from 1956–58) won the National Book Award, Mark Halperin (1966 M.F.A.) won the United States Award of the International Poetry Forum, Maura Stanton (1971 M.F.A.) was chosen for the Yale Series, and David St. John (1974 M.F.A.) was a winner in the Discovery Contest. In 1976, Charles E. Poverman (1969 M.F.A.) won the Iowa School of Letters Award for Short Fiction, Larry Levis (1974 M.F.A.) won the Lamont, and Joe Haldeman (1975 M.F.A.) won the Hugo Award (for best science fiction novel of the year). In 1978, James Alan McPherson (1971 M.F.A.) won a Pulitzer Prize for Fiction, in 1979 Leslie Ullman (1974 M.F.A.) was awarded the Yale Series, and in 1980 Donald Justice (1954 Ph.D.) won a Pulitzer Prize for Poetry.

The Workshop Experience

PARTICIPATING in a program like the Iowa Writers' Workshop can be as exhilarating and inspiring as it can be stifling and discouraging. Depending on individual temperament and needs, a writer might flourish from the association with other writers or flounder from the pressure of competition. Those who profit from their participation in the program at Iowa commonly cite the benefits of an environment in which writing is taken seriously and in which time is made available for writing, while those who do not profit often point to the damaging effects of unsympathetic criticism and to loss of artistic identity.

The question of teaching creative writing, and of learning to write in an academic setting, has been hotly debated in recent years. Because the university has become an important patron of the artist in American culture, the issue is significant. Nelson Algren, who once taught at Iowa, has written, ". . . the Writers' Workshop provides sanctuary from those pressures in which creativity is forged. If you want to create something of your own, stay away."[1] Robert Bly, a reluctant graduate of the Iowa program, has expressed his concern over the fact that writers who associate themselves with universities are robbed of the loneliness which is necessary for meaningful creative expression.[2] Traditionally, writers have been suspicious of any arrangement which links the artist with the establishment or renders him as something less than a free agent in society.

The idea of teaching or learning the art of writing as one might teach or learn mathematics may be repugnant to those who view art as the product of unfettered genius. But the majority of writers who have taught at the Iowa Writers' Workshop do not believe that writing can be "taught" or "learned" in the strict sense of these words. In a recent interview, Vance Bourjaily commented:

> I think I should make a distinction between teaching and learning. I can't *teach* anybody to be a writer, but somebody might come in here and *learn* to be a writer. Now, the learning that goes on, goes on for many reasons. It goes on because of the exchanges that students have with their peers and colleagues. For some, learning may be ac-

complished by being in a student-teacher relationship with an older, established writer and he or she is able to articulate for that particular student certain things that make sense.[3]

Like Bourjaily, Donald Justice does not claim that he "teaches" his students how to write. When interviewed, he explained:

> . . . "teach" is perhaps too direct and uncomplicated a verb for what may happen. What I want to suggest is that it would be very hard to prescribe a set of rules by which writing can be accomplished by writers or by teachers of writing. You work privately with a person as much as you can and as profitably for both of you as you can without having in mind certain dogmas, certain prescriptions, and certain rules. You learn then from your best students the things you hadn't imagined beforehand so that with the very best students the teaching of writing also becomes the learning of writing.[4]

Marvin Bell agrees that writing cannot be "taught," but he believes that "you can teach a kind of professionalism in the good sense," an attitude which he defines as "being able to think seriously about one's art, rather than being a quivering mass of talent." He observed:

> The best thing we do, I think, is to create an atmosphere of friendliness and respect for the art. That doesn't always work for every person at every time. There're people who feel so paranoid about being here that they feel it's a really unfriendly place. Some people benefit by feeling that they're fighting everyone. They fight the Workshop all the way. They go home every single night saying, "Those sons of bitches don't understand me and don't appreciate me," and they grow *that* way. Other people don't benefit at all and just turn around and leave. But most people, I think, would agree that it's pretty much a friendly place, that people respect people for being writers or at least don't hold it against them.
>
> So we try to create an atmosphere in which people can talk to one another about their work and about their reading and criticize one another's work, criticize one another, support one another, and learn from one another. Then of course there's a certain amount of this that is official in a sense—that is when we get together in the classes and discuss students' poems, when students ask for conferences with teachers and sit alone with them and discuss poems with them. And I think that you try this or that or read this or that. To a great extent, learning to write is done by learning to read, by reading good work. One of the things we always try to do is to say to people, "Have you read such and such? I think you would enjoy such and such."[5]

By and large, the writers who have made up the faculty of the Workshop have not forgotten the overriding importance of genius. As "teachers" of writing, they might help others to master the elements of their craft, but they make no attempt to teach talent.

In considering the benefits and shortcomings of writing programs like the Iowa Workshop, it is important to keep in mind that individual artists have widely differing needs. For some, the university will never be the right place. Of these writers, Paul Engle has written:

> They should remain on the road or on the beach or up in the attic or down in the cellar. It's a big country, mister. There's a place for everybody, in or out of the university, in or out of the house, in or out of jail.[6]

Even for those who are suited temperamentally to work well in groups, the Workshop might prove helpful only at certain times in their development or in their lives.

For many writers who have come to Iowa, the atmosphere of serious endeavor has been the most important aspect of their experience. Constance Urdang (who came to Iowa City in 1954) wrote:

> What I value the Iowa Workshop for is the time it gave me to write. The opportunity to do my own work in my own way. The coming together of a number of writers and would-be writers in one place. The people to talk to about writing, and about what and where and when to "send out." None of this took place in the weekly meeting—many people never went to those, anyway; but without the Workshop none of it would or could have happened.
>
> The Workshop was a focus. It created an expectation in yourself that you would write. It took your writing seriously. And it took the idea of writing seriously, seriously.[7]

Joe Bellamy (who was awarded an M.F.A. in 1969) has described his reaction to the seriousness in purpose that he encountered at Iowa in this way:

> What mattered for me was here was a place where to be a writer was not considered crazy or stupid. It was considered a serious life, and people were actually living that life and managing to do it. Writing had been a kind of traumatic ideal for me so to see that it was real for others was very important.[8]

For James Tate (1967 M.F.A.), attending the Workshop was a "hell of a sudden and thorough baptism into a new consciousness of the contemporary world of poetry." Before his stay in Iowa he had met few other writers, which had made it difficult to develop artistically. But at Iowa he discovered an environment that offered support and incentive:

It occurred to me that in my class there were an awfully lot of other writers who had come from different parts of the country and who were in the same stage of development as myself. It didn't matter what age they were. Suddenly they found themselves quite committed to following through as writers.[9]

Gail Godwin (who was awarded an M.A. in 1968 and a Ph.D. in 1971) recalled being "dropped out of the airplane in the middle of nowhere," and finding "for once everyone around me totally concerned with writing." She described the effect that this attitude had on her as a writer:

I had never been in a situation like that before, a situation where I had to take myself seriously, both because I had the time, the space, the quiet, and because other people around me were writing. So I came of age there. I blossomed. I finally got down to writing. I became a professional writer at Iowa.

The first spring I was there I found it all so stimulating that I began staying up all night and writing. Then I would sleep in the daytime until two o'clock. I found it exciting to be alone at night with the radio on—there was a program that would go on all night—and there would be snow outside. For the first time, I felt that I was alone with what mattered. It was not only the writing and the people who were writers that impressed me. It was also the place, this mythical place with all its ghosts of famous writers from the past. In the wintertime it's like a blank page.[10]

Likewise, John Engels (who participated in the program in 1956–57) observed, "Iowa and the workshops are so much a part of my life that I cannot conceive of what it might have been like without them," and Tess Gallagher (who came in 1972) has described her stay in Iowa City as "the busiest, most productive time of my life."[11] Thrilled by the constant and continuing discussions of poetry, Peter Everwine (who came to Iowa in 1954 after having served in the army) began writing desperately in order to have material for the workshop sessions, and John Irving, who lived in Iowa City as a student (1965–67) and instructor (1972–74), wrote (at least in part) three of his four published works. Bruce Dobler (who participated in the program in 1966–68) believes not only that the Workshop saved him five or ten years' time in development, but that Iowa's practice of offering academic credit and advanced degrees for writing legitimizes in the eyes of the outside world the writer's period of apprenticeship:

The attitude of the teachers and the structure of the program made it easy for me to go from part-time writing, writing as a hobby, to a full-time commitment to a craft. And that kind of commitment, which the

Workshop fosters, is necessary. And, really doesn't a writer in our society need that built-in excuse, for himself and for others? Suppose I had announced to friends, family, in-laws that I was going to sit back and write for two or three years while my wife worked full-time and we borrowed whatever else we needed to get by. I could have done that—but at what a cost. So instead, we did just what I described and all the family and friends thought it was just great. Bruce went back to get a graduate degree. I know this sounds simpleminded, but when you come right down to it, I can't think of a better way for a person to put a good face on dropping out to just write for a few years. Especially for someone from a working class family. So that was one big thing the Workshop did. It provided the setting for commitment to writing and a solid alibi for the world.[12]

For many, the experience of living in close vicinity with other aspiring writers has been both stimulating and disillusioning. Marvin Bell described this mixed reaction in an interview:

> . . . when you have a big community of writers like this set in a little midwestern town, it's difficult to go on pretending that you're terribly special or visionary. Everybody knows you struck out in the softball game yesterday and you fell down the stairs Friday and that your child was yelling during the movie. I mean, everybody knows and so you gradually stop pretending you're just a great artist of some kind. That's a real advantage, I think. The ego of young writers gets in the way of perception. There's just *so much* ego and personality in the way of perception and anything that can counteract that is good. I think just the Midwest setting and the fact that there are so many writers around here does counteract that, and I think that's healthy.[13]

Dobler was one who adopted a more realistic and sober view regarding the writer's dream of fame:

> When I punched tickets on the IC suburban trains I used to wonder what it would be like to be published. Then I came to Iowa and saw that it wasn't anything, really. You still had to wait in line at stores, people didn't call after you on the street. You didn't do anything but just live and work and try to get something else started. It made it a lot easier for me not to be carried away either by excitement or disappointment when I got published. The dream was real and I could see it and I got used to it. You can't believe that there's anything so mysterious about being a writer when you come to that first session and meet ninety other people who have the same dream. I don't know if I make myself clear, but I was glad to be in a place where people were hungry to make it, but at the same time—well, they were a dime a dozen.[14]

The workshop sessions constitute the heart of the program. It is here that much of the business of "learning" to write takes place. But often the experience of opening oneself up for criticism is simply too intense. Flannery O'Connor (1947 M.F.A.) was perhaps recalling the workshop sessions at Iowa when she commented, "Every time a story of mine appears in a freshman anthology, I have a vision of it, with its little organs laid open, like a frog in a bottle."[15] Rella Lossy (who attended the Workshop in 1952–53) has vivid memories of these sessions:

> The most threatening part of it was that the chairs lined the walls, and some victim was left to knock around in the terrible empty accusing space in the middle of the room. I always went to workshop feeling like a fraud.

In spite of the fact that "it all mattered" to her, after a year and a half of workshopping Lossy "ran home to Chicago and got a safe 9 to 5 job."[16]

A number of graduates have criticized the workshop sessions for being too negative in tone, and have felt that a lack of sympathy as well as a lack of constructive commentary existed in the Workshop. Bruce Dobler was dismayed by "the bickering of students, the constant biting and clawing," of which he himself was "guilty":

> I sensed that a great many students did not come to Iowa with an open spirit and a desire to apprentice themselves to journeymen writers. They came full of themselves (a charitable way to put it) and wanted only to be appreciated for what they already knew. They were resistant to learning and teaching—self expressers for the most part who were only looking for uncritical love. Since they didn't get it, they poured invective on their fellows in class. . . . I remember a short story by Gail Godwin, probably the best-known of my peers at Iowa. It has a tramp in it who rapes an American librarian in London. The men in the class were tearing the story up, particularly critical of the tramp. Lucy Rosenthal, who is an editor with the Book-of-the-month-club-magazine (and who gave Gail a great review last month) said, "Well I thought the tramp *qua* tramp was *very* well drawn." A male voice came back in imitation. "I thought the tramp *qua* tramp was shit *qua* shit."[17]

Along these same lines, Phil Hey (1966 M.F.A.) faulted the sessions for their "cynicism toward freedom and inventiveness." He explained:

> It seemed that attitudinal matters were not often considered, that the psychology of the poet/poem/audience were not worth serious attention; rather, it seemed that everyone was trying to resolve all problems of poetry into technical ones. It can't be done. One result was what

everyone calls the "workshop poem," which has nothing to say but says it well, elegantly, awarely, foolproof. So, there was not enough concern about what there really is to say, and who the sayer is. In somewhat the same vein, the Workshop still *schooled* its students, much as it probably didn't want to, to write for the teachers and each other. The object seemed sometimes not poetry (or, heaven forbid, truth), but technical superiority, impressing your classmate, writing ironclad attack-proof poems. I know, I was one who did just that. [18]

Patricia Hampl has generally good feelings about her stay at Iowa, but she too was distressed by what she perceived to be a lack of openness:

It was, artistically, an isolating experience. [There was] very little contact among poets and fiction writers, for one thing. And even more unfortunate (because of the opportunities missed), [there was] very little contact between the regular Workshop and the International Workshop (where people generally stay only one year and therefore are gone soon). . . . I was unhappy as a woman, to find myself (especially my first year, 68–69) in a crushing minority; and later, as a white person, felt frustrated and appalled to discover that sometimes faculty and students had no concept of the humility requisite when approaching new or "foreign" (as black, Indian or Chicano literature can actually be) work. I was disappointed because I hated to see the words "high standards" used as unwitting code words for lack of real curiosity and eagerness for this literature. [19]

In the same vein, William Stafford (who attended the Workshop in the early fifties) worries that belonging to a group can stifle the writer's desire to experiment:

I think the disadvantage inherent in any gathering like this, where you are implicitly in competition, is that a person will begin to compete with the conscious mind by means of techniques and maneuvers and will turn loose of what is really essential, I think, for an artist or writer, and that is a willingness to fail, a willingness to try things, a relaxation to let your own life dominate your own writing. It's almost inevitable that surrounded by successful people you will emulate them, you will choose their topics, you will follow their style, and I think it's dangerous. [20]

Nearly every participant has sensed and reacted with some apprehension to a spirit of competition in the Workshop setting. But many writers view the ordeal of measuring their talent against the talent of others as a necessary crisis in their artistic development. Paul Engle believes that the intensity of this experience contributes to the writer's growth:

In the process of original writing, every word and every attitude is subject to a constant scrutiny, or should be, and much of what we do is to heighten the sense of awareness which this requires. We knock, or persuade, or terrify, the false tenderness toward his own work out of the beginning writer. This is the beginning of wisdom.[21]

When asked about the element of competition and how it might work for or against a writer, John Leggett responded:

For the most part I think that it works in his favor, but, sure, I *have* seen people who freeze up here if they feel that they're doing something different from the general run of Workshop students and if they try a worksheet, particularly if it's obscure or difficult, and they're badly beaten in the workshop. I've seen people freeze up. I've seen them dry up and not be able to stand to be here. I've seen people, who are neurotic to begin with, become even more so and find that they just can't stay here. It's too much for them. But that's fairly rare.

When the Workshop does work and does effectively help a student, it is because of the stimulus of a writer having an audience made up of the, say, twelve or fourteen students of his or her class. I think that a member of such a group—when there are four or five people in that circle whose work he admires—tends to write at his very best. It is very much akin to publication, to the sense of immediacy about publication that as you are writing or typing up a piece you know that next Tuesday people will be getting to know you better and perhaps getting to admire what it is that you are doing. It tends to make you write to the top of your form.[22]

In spite of his reservations about writing programs, William Stafford believes that he benefited from learning to bear up under criticism:

I learned that it was possible to survive and that even the sternest critics were vulnerable themselves. You don't learn that unless you confront them. And I began to have this feeling, whether justifiably or not, that writers are, sure, people with opinions and talents, but also weaknesses and that I was one of them. I mean I just began to feel, "Yes, I'm a writer." You know, a writer is a person who writes. I'm writing. Everyone goes through the same mill I do at these workshops. I was able to be in the presence of flourishing people who could write well, like Jim Hall and like Don Justice and others, and they could be frank and direct, but not utterly annihilating. And I survived. And it made me have a feeling—like undergoing a gruelling course—if I can survive the Iowa Workshop I can survive anything. So by the time I finished I felt confident about writing and about living with other writers.[23]

For Joe Bellamy, the intensity of the experience instilled in him a lasting desire to write:

> My actual years at Iowa were fairly uncomfortable. It was only after I left Iowa that I looked back and saw the experience as a positive one.
>
> It seems to me that the Workshop is set up like a pressure cooker, with a rigid status system depending on publication, and you step into this system and you find that here is a world where, if you publish, you have status. If you do not publish, you have no status. And those who haven't published usually feel pretty dismal. So in a kind of Pavlovian way, it sets up an intense desire to publish, a hunger for it.[24]

Jack Myers (who attended the Workshop in 1970–72) described his response to the pressure in this way:

> Because the rewards in both the workshop and literary scene are relatively so few, there was an intense competitive spirit underlying the life of the workshop. I had a family and was determined to win a teaching assistantship by writing and revising day and night. I know other poets there were just as determined as me. This competition did sour some students on the workshop experience. I think they felt that competition had no place in the life of an artist and their work and egoes suffered under the severe pressure of trying to survive in this atmosphere. But most of the poets I knew thrived in the excited literary environment. They learned to drink just as deeply to failure as to success, because I think we all felt that we were really only pitting ourselves against our last best effort.[25]

Even those writers who were more often miserable than happy while participating in the Writers' Workshop have discovered the advantages of having joined a community which extends beyond the bounds of Iowa City. The sense of belonging to a group, of living together in a larger society and working for a common purpose, can be as reassuring as the threat of competition can be stifling. Constance Urdang has written of this spirit of camaraderie: "Whether or not we ever see each other these days, I continue to count among my real friends many of the writers I met in Iowa City. In an odd way, we can depend on each other."[26] The feeling of belonging, in the opinion of Charles Poverman, creates a common bond among the graduates of the Workshop:

> The community remains intact. I mean, the people who cared about each other still follow each other's work. The community isn't limited to the time and space that you're in Iowa City. . . . We've had an experience in common and we know what it was. . . . It's like a residue.[27]

On a more practical level, belonging to the Workshop community gives a writer contacts with members of the larger literary establishment—not only with other writers but with literary agents, editors, publishers, critics and reviewers. In the academic world, a writer with a degree from Iowa might stand a better chance of being hired as a teacher than another writer with otherwise equivalent credentials. While contacts may not advance a writer who lacks talent, they can be invaluable to the unknown but talented writer who must face overwhelming odds in the battle to establish a reputation. In the words of Daniel Marder (1950 M.F.A.), "The importance of the Workshop to American letters lies in its connections. It tends to create a kind of literary establishment not with a strong core as in New York but as a network of fibers with sense endings everywhere."[28]

It is too early to assess the ultimate significance of the Iowa Writers' Workshop to twentieth-century American letters. But it is obvious that writing programs like the Workshop have become for the writer in American society an important form of patronage. They fill a void left by the disappearance of editors who really worked with writers, as Maxwell Perkins worked with Fitzgerald and Wolfe. In the absence of the old-style editors, developing writers have turned to writing programs for support and encouragement. In the same way, programs like the Writers' Workshop have become centers for writers living in a country that has no London or Paris—and no longer has Boston or Concord, Greenwich Village or San Francisco—as its literary capital. "Since we don't have café tables in the United States and there's no longer a community like Greenwich Village was in the twenties," Robie Macauley (1950 M.F.A.) remarked recently, "the Iowa Workshop is the next best thing. It's a university center with enough money and enthusiasm to bring artists together."[29] Paul Engle no doubt had all of this in mind when he wrote: "It is conceivable that by the end of the twentieth century the American university will have proved a more understanding and helpful aid to literature than even the old families of Europe."[30]

NOTES

1   Nelson Algren, "At play in the fields of hack-ademe," *Chicago Tribune Magazine* (October 21, 1973). This material also appears in *The Last Carousel* (New York: Putnam, 1973), pp. 74–82.

2   Stephen Wilbers, "Robert Bly Returns," *prairie grass*, 3 (February 1, 1978).

---

3 "Inside the Iowa Writers' Workshop: Interviews with Donald Justice, Marvin Bell, and Vance Bourjaily," *North American Review*, 262 (Summer 1977), 15.

4 *Ibid.*, 7.

5 *Ibid.*, 11.

6 Paul Engle, "Introduction: The Writer and the Place," *Midland, An Anthology of Poetry and Prose*, edited by Paul Engle with assistance from Henri Coulette and Donald Justice (New York: Random House, 1961), p. xxxi.

7 Constance Urdang, letter to the author, February 27, 1976, "Workshop Correspondence with Wilbers," no. 42, University of Iowa Archives, Iowa City.

8 Wilbers, "Looking Back on the Iowa Pressure Cooker," *Iowa Alumni Review*, 30 (February/March 1977), 7.

9 *Ibid.*

10 *Ibid.*

11 John Engels, letter to the author, undated, "Workshop Correspondence with Wilbers," no. 43, University of Iowa Archives, Iowa City. Tess Gallagher was interviewed by the author at the 1976 St. Lawrence Writers' Conference at Lake Saranac.

12 Bruce Dobler, letter to the author, April 30, 1976, "Workshop Correspondence with Wilbers," no. 130, University of Iowa Archives, Iowa City.

13 Wilbers, "Inside the Iowa Writers' Workshop," 12.

14 Dobler, no. 130.

15 Jean Wylder, "Flannery O'Connor: A Reminiscence and Some Letters," *North American Review*, 255 (Spring 1970), 58.

16 Rella Lossy, letter to the author, October 11, 1976, "Workshop Correspondence with Wilbers," no. 243, University of Iowa Archives, Iowa City.

17 Dobler, letter to the author, no. 130.

18 Phil Hey, letter to the author, acknowledged May 28, 1976, "Workshop Correspondence with Wilbers," no. 119, University of Iowa Archives, Iowa City.

19 Patricia Hampl, letter to the author, May 25, 1976, "Workshop Correspondence with Wilbers," no. 164, University of Iowa Archives, Iowa City.

20 William Stafford, in an interview with the author, April 20, 1976, Iowa City.

21 Engle, p. xxiv.

22 Wilbers, "Interview with Jack Leggett," *prairie grass*, 1 (April 1, 1977).

23 Stafford, interview, April 20, 1976.

24 Wilbers, "Looking Back on the Iowa Pressure Cooker," 6.

25 Jack Myers, letter to the author, May 18, 1976, "Workshop Correspondence with Wilbers," no. 153, University of Iowa Archives, Iowa City.

26 Urdang, letter to the author, no. 42.

27 Wilbers, "Looking Back on the Iowa Pressure Cooker," 6.

28 Daniel Marder, letter to the author, April 30, 1976, "Workshop Correspondence with Wilbers," no. 122, University of Iowa Archives, Iowa City.

29 Wilbers, "Looking Back on the Iowa Pressure Cooker," 7.

30 Engle, p. xxx.

Appendix
Writing Programs Founded or Directed by Iowa Workshop Graduates

MANY Iowa Workshop graduates presently hold teaching positions in American colleges and universities. Although they are too numerous to mention here, it *is* possible to give an account (by no means complete) of the programs founded and presently directed by former Workshop students. This is not to imply that these programs were all modeled after the Iowa Writers' Workshop, but to demonstrate that there is at least some connection between Iowa and a significant number of writing programs in this country.

In 1960, the only programs really competing with the Iowa Workshop were those at the University of Denver (which like Iowa was awarding the Ph.D. for a creative dissertation), and at Stanford, Michigan, Indiana, and Hollins in Virginia (which were awarding creative M.A.s). Of the latter, the University of Michigan now allows an option in creative writing for the doctorate. In addition to Iowa and Michigan, the following programs presently allow creative dissertations for the Ph.D.: the University of California at Santa Cruz (which permits one-third of the dissertation to be creative and whose faculty includes James B. Hall, founding provost of College V, a program permitting a major in aesthetic studies); the University of Denver (directed by Robert Pawlowski); the University of Southern Mississippi (directed by Bernard Kaplan); the University of South Carolina (whose staff includes Dan Marin); Texas Tech University (founded and directed by Walter McDonald); and the University of Utah (whose staff includes Harold Moore and once included in the program's early stage Wallace Stegner). All of the faculty members mentioned above are graduates of the Iowa program.

Of the programs offering a Master of Fine Arts degree, the following were either founded or are presently directed by Iowa graduates: the University of Alabama (whose M.F.A. program, but not its earlier M.A. program, was founded by its present director, Thomas Rabbitt); the University of Arkansas (co-founded by William Harrison and James Whitehead); Bowling Green State University (one of whose founders was Philip O'Connor); the University of California at Irvine (one of whose founders was James B. Hall and whose present director is Oakley Hall); the University of Northern Iowa (whose founder was Loren Taylor); the University of Massachusetts at Amherst (whose co-founders include Joseph Langland, Andrew Fetler, Richard Kim, and Robert Tucker); the University of Montana (one of whose founders was John Hermann); the University of Oregon (whose founder was James B. Hall and whose present director is Richard Lyons); and Wichita State University (co-founded by Bruce Cutler and Philip Scheider). Once again, all the faculty members listed are graduates of the Iowa Workshop.

Of the programs offering a Master of Arts degree, the following were either founded or are presently directed by Iowa graduates: Bemidji State University (founded and directed by William D. Elliott); Brown University (directed by Michael S. Harper); California State University at Long Beach (one of whose founders was John Hermann, presently a staff member); the University of Chicago (founded and directed by Richard G. Stern); Humboldt State University (directed by Richard C. Day); the University of Louisville (directed by Sena Jeter Naslund); Central Michigan University at Mount Pleasant (one of whose founders was Eric Torgersen, presently a faculty member); Colorado State University (founded by James Crumley); San Francisco State University (directed by William Dickey); Stanford University (founded by Wallace Stegner); Southwest Texas State University (founded and directed by Norman Peterson); Vanderbilt University (founded and directed by Walter Sullivan); Central Washington University (one of whose founders was Mark Halperin, presently a faculty member); Eastern Washington University (one of whose founders was Jerry Bumpus); Western Washington University (founded by Knute Skinner); University of Wisconsin at Milwaukee (one of whose founders was Morgan Gibson). In addition, one of the oldest undergraduate programs in the country (at the University of Pittsburgh) was founded in part by Percival Hunt, who graduated from Iowa with a B.A. in 1902 and who taught the Iowa course in short story writing for two decades before going to Pittsburgh.

Of the programs offering an undergraduate emphasis in creative writing, the following were either founded or are presently directed by Iowa graduates: St. Lawrence University (founded and directed by Joe David Bellamy); Lock Haven State College (co-founded by Vincent Stewart and Joseph Nicholson, both present staff members); Western Michigan University (two of whose founders were Herbert Scott and Stuart Dybek); State University of New York College at Oswego (founded and directed by Lewis Turco); and Pennsylvania State University (two of whose founders were Daniel Marder and S. Leonard Rubinstein, who is present director of the writing option).

In addition to the above listings, Harry Barba founded the program at Skidmore College and at Marshall University served as director of writing and coordinator of a $100,000 Title I Writing Arts Program in Appalachia; Edilberto and Edith Tiempo founded in 1961 the National Writers' Workshop at Silliman University in the Philippines, the first writing program in Asia; Edmund Skellings has served as director of the Alaska Writers' Workshop and is presently executive director of the International Institute for Creative Communication at Florida International University; Robert Williams (a former faculty member at Iowa) founded and presently directs the program at California State University at Hayward, which he designed and set up while teaching at Iowa; and George Starbuck (the third director of the Iowa Workshop) presently directs the program at Boston University.

Information here (compiled in the spring of 1976) is based on the results of a survey that was mailed to 125 universities and colleges. The pool of writing programs was compiled from the *CEA Chap Book* (1970), the *Associated Writing Programs* 1975 *Catalog of Programs (including the directory at the end)*, and an "in-house" list of thirty-two programs that the Iowa Writers' Workshop staff recognizes as "top" programs.

In addition to the founders and directors listed here, many Iowa Workshop graduates serve as faculty to these and other programs. For some of their names, consult the folder entitled "Writers' Workshop: Survey," University of Iowa Archives, Iowa City, Iowa.

Bibliography

Alexander, Margaret Walker. *How I Wrote Jubilee.* Chicago: Third World Press, 1972.

Algren, Nelson. "At play in the fields of hack-ademe." *Chicago Tribune Magazine,* October 21, 1973.

————. *The Last Carousel.* New York: Putnam, 1973.

Andrews, Clarence A. *A Literary History of Iowa.* Iowa City: University of Iowa Press, 1972.

Ansley, Delight. "Clarke Fisher Ansley." New York: Columbia University Press, June 1974.

————. *First Chronicles.* Doylestown, Penn.: Gardy Printing, 1971.

"Edwin Ford Piper Papers." Iowa City: University of Iowa Archives.

"Frank Luther Mott Papers." Iowa City: University of Iowa Archives.

"Norman Foerster Papers." Iowa City: University of Iowa Archives.

"Presidents' Correspondence," various years. Iowa City: University of Iowa Archives.

"Workshop Correspondence with Wilbers." Iowa City: University of Iowa Archives.

"Writers' Workshop: Reminiscences." Iowa City: University of Iowa Archives.

"Writers' Workshop: Survey." Iowa City: University of Iowa Archives.

"Athens in the Cornfields." *Esquire,* 53 (1960):6.

Baker, Joseph E. and Beath, Paul Robert. "Regionalism: Pro and Con; Four Arguments for Regionalism and Four Fallacies of Regionalism." *Saturday Review of Literature* (November 28, 1936):3.

Baker, Mary Jane. "Classes with a Poet." *Mademoiselle,* 40 (1954):106.

Boroff, David. "The Muses Meet in Squaresville." *Mademoiselle,* 54 (1961):106.

Brigham, Johnson. "Iowa's Strategic Position. A Talk with Broad-Gauge Advertisers." *Midland Monthly,* 4 (1895).

Bush, Jr., Sargent. "The Achievement of John T. Frederick." *Books at Iowa,* 14 (1971):8–30.

Cook, Jr., Louis. "Sam Sloan, Teacher Extraordinary, Retires to His Flowers." *Des Moines Register,* April 30, 1939.

Davis, Hallie Flanagan. *Arena.* New York: Duell, Sloan and Pearce, 1940.

"Eggheads in the Tall Corn." *Newsweek* (December 28, 1959):65–66.

Engle, Paul. "Introduction: The Writer and the Place." *Midland: An Anthology of Poetry and Prose.* Ed. by Paul Engle with assistance from Henri Coulette and Donald Justice. New York: Random House, 1961.

Flanagan, Frances Mary. "The Educational Role of Norman Foerster." Ph.D. dissertation, University of Iowa, 1971.

Foerster, Norman. *The American Scholar.* Chapel Hill: University of North Carolina Press, 1929.

————. *Literature and the Art of Writing.* Iowa City: State University of Iowa Press, 1936–37.

Frederick, John T. "The First Person Plural." *Midland,* 1 (1915):1–2.

————. "A Maker of Songs." *American Prefaces,* 2 (1937):83–84.

————. "The Younger School." *Palimpsest,* 12 (1931):78–86.

Glaspell, Susan. *The Road to the Temple.* New York: Frederick A. Stokes, 1927.

Godwin, Gail. "The Iowa Experience." *New Times* (January 10, 1975):48.

Hamlin Garland's Diaries. Ed. by Donald Pizer. San Marino: Huntington Library, 1968.

Hansen, Harry. "The Iowa Writers' Conference." *Saturday Review of Literature* (November 21, 1931):315.

Harris, T. George. "University of Iowa's Paul Engle, Poet-Grower to the World." *Look* (June 1, 1965):95–97.

Hawkeye. Yearbook of the University of Iowa, Iowa City, various issues.

Hills, L. Rust. "The Structure of the American Literary Establishment." *Esquire,* 60 (1963):41–43.

————. "A Town of Many Talents." *Saturday Review* (July 1, 1961), 12–13.

Homage to Baudelaire. Ed. by Paul Engle. Iowa City: Cummington Press, 1957.

Hunt, Percival. *If by Your Art, Testament to Percival Hunt.* Pittsburgh: University of Pittsburgh Press, 1948.

"Iowa's School of Letters Admits Imaginative, Critical Writing for Ph.D. Thesis." *Daily Iowan,* March 26, 1931.

Kentfield, Calvin. "State University of Iowa" *Holiday,* 34 (1963):88.

Marshall, Max Lawrence. *Frank Luther Mott: Journalism Educator.* Ph.D. dissertation, University of Missouri, 1968.

McPeak, Ivan. "Historical, 1913–1918." *Athelney Book,* 5 (1918):7.

Mott, Frank Luther. "Literature with Roots." *Midland,* 19 (1932):82–84.

————. "The Midland." *Palimpsest,* 43 (1962):133–44.

————. "The Midland" and "The S.P.C.S." *Time Enough: Essays in Autobiography.* Chapel Hill: University of North Carolina Press, 1962.

————. "The S.P.C.S." *Palimpsest,* 43 (1962):113–32.

"New Man, New Iowa." *Time* (September 23, 1940):42–43.

O'Brien, Edward J. *Best Short Stories of 1930.* Boston: Houghton Mifflin, 1930.

Ohnstad, Karsten. *The World at My Finger Tips.* Indianapolis & New York: Bobbs-Merrill, 1942.

Oster, Harry. "The Edwin Ford Piper Collection of Folksongs." *Books at Iowa,* 1 (1964):28–33.

Petersen, Clarence. *Chicago Sun-Times Magazine,* April 28, 1968, p. 34.

"Poets on the Farm." *Time* (June 3, 1957), 39.

Polking, Kirk. "Creative Education." *Writers' Digest* (1962):17–22.

Reigelman, Milton M. *The Midland: A Venture in Literary Regionalism.* Iowa City: University of Iowa Press, 1975.
Roth, Philip. "Iowa, A Very Far Country Indeed." *Esquire,* 58 (1962):132.
Royce, Josiah. "Provincialism." *Race Questions, Provincialism, and other American Problems.* New York: Macmillan, 1908.

Schramm, Wilbur. "Approaches to a Science of English Verse." *University of Iowa Studies, Series on Aims and Progress of Research, 46* (1935).
_____. *The Story Workshop.* Boston: Little, Brown, 1938.
_____. "Imaginative Writing." *Literary Scholarship, Its Aims and Methods.* Ed. by Norman Foerster, John C. McGalliard, René Wellek, Austin Warren, and Wilbur L. Schramm. Chapel Hill: University of North Carolina Press, 1941.
Seashore, Carl and Wilbur Schramm. "Time and Intensity in English Tetrameter Verse." *Philological Quarterly,* 13 (1934):65.
Sloan, Sam B. "Misrepresentative Fiction." *Palimpsest,* 12 (1931): 41.
"The State University of Iowa." *Time* (September 6, 1954):59.
Stegner, Wallace. "New Climates for the Writer." *The Writer in America.* Osaka: Hokuseido Press, 1951.
_____. "The Trail of the Hawkeye, Literature Where the Tall Corn Grows." *Saturday Review of Literature* (July 30, 1938):3.
Suckow, Ruth. "Iowa." *American Mercury,* 9 (1926):39–45.
"The Summer Writers' Workshop." Iowa City: University of Iowa Publications, April 16, 1941. Copy in University of Iowa Archives.

Tanselle, G. Thomas. "George Cram Cook and the Poetry of Living, with a Checklist." *Books at Iowa,* 24 (April 1976):3.
Theses and Dissertations, presented in the graduate college of the State University of Iowa, 1900–1950. Compiled by Sarah Scott Edwards and ed. by Pauline Cook. Iowa City, 1952.

University of Iowa Catalogue. Various issues.
University of Iowa News Bulletin, 16 (1914).

Wallace, Una. "A Singing Professor." *Daily Iowan,* Sunday Magazine Section, December 6, 1931.
Walljasper, Jay. *"Defender,* dawn of underground press." *Daily Iowan,* November 29, 1976.
Wanerus, Theodore. *The History of The Zetagathian Society.* Iowa City: Zetagathian Society, 1911.
Weaver, James B. "The Authors' Homecoming of 1914." *Midland,* 1 (1915):22–25.
Weber, Irving. *Iowa City.* Iowa City: Iowa City Lions Club, 1976.
Wilbers, Stephen. "Inside the Iowa Writers' Workshop: Interviews with Donald Justice, Marvin Bell, and Vance Bourjaily." *North American Review,* 262 (1977): 7–15.
_____. "Interview with Jack Leggett." *prairie grass,* 1 (1977).
_____. "The Iowa City Writers' Clubs." *Palimpsest,* 59 (1978):44–57.
_____. "Looking Back on the Iowa Pressure Cooker." *Iowa Alumni Review,* 30 (1977):6–7.

————. "Paul Engle: An Imaginative and Delicate Aggression." *Iowa Alumni Review*, 30 (1977):8–13.

————. "Robert Bly Returns." *prairie grass*, 3 (1978).

Wood, Grant. "A Definition of Regionalism." *Books at Iowa*, 3 (1965):3–4.

————. *Revolt Against the City*. Whirling World Series 1. Iowa City: Clio Press, 1935.

Wylder, Jean. "Flannery O'Connor: A Reminiscence and Some Letters." *North American Review*, 255 (1970):58–65.

————. Interview with John T. Frederick. University of Iowa Workshop Archives.

Youmans, Ardath. "Professor Sloan Recalls Days at S.U.I." *Daily Iowan*, May 20, 1948.

"Young Writers Are Producing in S.U.I. Workshop." *University of Iowa News Bulletin*, 16 (1941).

INDEX